The Pocket Essential

UFOs

www.pocketessentials.com

First published in Great Britain 2002 by Pocket Essentials, 18 Coleswood Road, Harpenden, Herts, AL5 1EQ

Distributed in the USA by Trafalgar Square Publishing, PO Box 257, Howe Hill Road, North Pomfret, Vermont 05053

Copyright © Neil Nixon 2002
Series Editor: Paul Duncan

A CIP catalogue record for this book is available from the British Library.

ISBN 1-903047-88-9

2 4 6 8 10 9 7 5 3 1

Book typeset by Pdunk
Printed and bound by Cox & Wyman

Dedicated to two women without whom this book, and my life as I know it, would not exist.

My wife Jane whose understanding of my UFO obsession is one of the many loving and selfless acts that keep our love alive. I love you Jane.

Jenny Randles, a persistent and dedicated researcher unafraid of the truth, and a worthy role model to anyone intent on making a contribution to UFO investigation.

CONTENTS

1. Introduction

One Of These Days We Might Be Smart Enough To Ask The Right Questions

UFO means Unidentified Flying Object. The term was originally coined along with several others like UAO (Unidentified Ariel Object) and Flying Saucer to describe unknown objects seen in the sky.

The late and much missed UFOlogist Leonard Stringfield once tried to capture the frustration of chasing the elusive evidence for crashed UFOs by titling a book chapter, 'The Search For Proof In A Squirrel's Cage.'[1] Stringfield's cutting analysis was lost to the world in 1993 but, from this distance, it is tempting to say that his estimate of the confusion and contradiction he experienced would barely do justice to today's situation. It is a complex subject. The truth is out there somewhere and some of it may be in this book but, to complicate matters, you and I would probably find differing truths.

Celebrated UFOlogist Dr J Allen Hynek[2] noted that UFOs are not studied. In reality, most of those with an active interest in UFOs only encounter verbal or written reports and reproduced images of the UFOs in question. This is true for both active investigators and armchair students of the subject. Put bluntly, UFOlogy is largely the study of secondary sources of evidence. This situation frequently leaves doubt in the minds of some as to whether the objects in question were ever genuinely unidentified and/or flying. And it gets more confusing! The term UFO on a book or video jacket has proven a sales winner time and again but much of the most marketable material in the last decade and a half has not been primarily concerned with flying objects at all. At the start of the 21st century UFO investigation and the popular market on the subject also include reports of other phenomena including: cattle mutilations; human abductions by aliens; people who claim to channel messages from aliens; and 'alternative archaeology,' which presents a revisionist view of history in which alien intelligences play a pivotal role in the history of life on this planet.

Central to all the strands of UFO investigation is that there is a series of phenomena that can be studied. Virtually all amateur UFO investigation assumes that there may be intelligence behind some of these phenomena. The most popular viewpoint amongst the subject's greatest supporters is that life alien to this planet is involved. There is certainly logic and rational thought behind these notions, but there is also much disagreement.

The truth about UFOs and UFO investigation is that a central core of mysterious reports are continually being appropriated and hijacked by people with their own agendas. The motivation behind this is often well meaning but the result has been to scatter the subject in a way that leaves entrenched camps seething with mutual suspicion and much research being undertaken in isolation. Information travels around, work is published and claims are made, but the major casualty is undisputed truth. The result is that many UFO cases of genuine substance are tainted by the shenanigans surrounding the investigations.

The many ironies are not lost on some of the key players. In recent years the British UFOlogist Andy Roberts[3] has unleashed the merciless and amusing newsletter *The Armchair UFOlogist*. His motto: 'Tough on UFOlogy, tough on the causes of UFOlogy.' This chronicle of political infighting and massive egos built on minuscule ideas casts UFOlogy as a collision between support groups for the socially wretched and an exercise in self-aggrandizement for a select group of the terminally delusional. Roberts' agenda is, in fact, very positive. His publication highlights the very real issue of the people problem that underpins much of the UFO world. Roberts' work reads like a detailed synopsis for the greatest movie Terry Gilliam could ever make. His message is that it doesn't have to be this way.

Put simply, it is very often impossible to separate the claims made about UFO events from the people who make these claims. The vast majority of UFO case investigation is amateur and the vast majority of investigators undergo a rudimentary initiation at best. It is easy to condemn the chaos and comedy that often result but there is little or no alternative. In a quiet year there are a few hundred UFO reports in the UK and no professional organisation exists to monitor, investigate and report on the situation.

There is some professional investigation ongoing, some of it producing vital and challenging work. However, the bad press attached to UFO investigation has left the subject in an academic limbo. On the one hand, UFO reports are fascinating and more substantial in terms of evidence than the cynics would like to admit. On the other hand, many employed in universities and colleges regard their amateur colleagues in UFO groups as a kind of Care In The Community branch of academia. The end result is predictable and tragic for the subject. UFO research has been seen as a certain route to career suicide for the best scientific and social scientific minds of several generations. Only a handful of serious, peer-reviewed studies exist. Research undertaken in Psychology, Tectonics and Sociology has made a substantial contribution to the UFO debate but it often fails to impress those involved in gathering field reports in their local area. In some cases those in research groups simply don't understand the academic research. In most cases, they get the gist of the ideas but, understandably, point out that it doesn't help them to explain anything to the terrified witness they've just interviewed. The most damning argument from the rank and file is also the most obvious. The academics who claim to study UFOs seldom do the local groundwork or meet the witnesses. Much academic work concerns itself with trying to replicate UFO events in laboratories. The academic fraternity for their part have often slammed the primitive and inaccurate investigative methods of the self-appointed research community of UFOlogy.

UFOlogy, a loose term coined to include pretty much any investigation related to UFO reports, is not a science. This was eloquently stated in a 1979 paper. NASA scientist James Oberg won a prize offered by Cutty Sark Whisky with his paper *The Failure Of The Science Of UFOlogy*.[4] Presenting himself as a benevolent sceptic, Oberg demolished the pretensions of the fledgling science with some substantial points. He saw UFOlogy as a protest movement, or the results of effective mythmaking. Almost twenty years later I followed up his report with a much longer investigation.[5] I found many of Oberg's points still applied, although the situation had become more complicated.

UFOlogy may not be a science. In fact it is no one thing. UFOs and the study of UFO events resemble, by turns, a protest movement, a branch of the entertainment industry, a collection of religious movements, a well-established scam for fleecing the public and a bizarre fringe profession employing a collection of visionaries and mavericks. The people problem may complicate the whole picture but we have to keep one truth in mind: UFOs and UFO investigation remain alive and well because, despite the problems, people continue to see and experience things they can't begin to explain.

Most of the people on the receiving end of such experiences did not ask for them and do not seek any publicity. They are, by turns, fascinated, frightened, changed as personalities and physically harmed. UFO cases may peak at times when UFOs are a popular media subject but they never go away. Many cases are easily explained. Some of the best-known are kept alive by a mixture of faith and bullshit but there are others so indisputably mysterious that they present a challenge to established ideas. The stories in this book include the terrifying, tragic and incredible. Honest sincere people report such things every day. Some of the possibilities presented by these cases are so awesome they strike at the very core of the deepest questions we can comprehend.

Your Guide

Hello, I'm Neil and I've been doing UFOs all my life. Having stated that people with an agenda hijack the information, I had better be honest about myself. Then I'll let the evidence do the talking.

The limitless imaginative possibilities of the stories got me involved in the field. Like most of my fellow UFOlogists I had it sussed within days. People were seeing alien spacecraft and anyone who disagreed was narrow-minded. Sorted! At this point I was around seven years old. Not long after that, I read the famous report of George Adamski's meeting with a man from Venus and thought 'Whaattt!!, maybe some of these stories aren't true.'

Since when I've remained true to the UFO cause and the pursuit of critical thinking. I've been part of investigation groups, stood on the stage at conferences and waded through a library of books even when their covers alone convinced me that the most reliable information inside was the publisher's address. I'm still here because this subject, in my opinion, is easily the greatest mystery of the modern age.

I am sceptical about most claims and I'm highly sceptical of evidence gathered using hypnotic regression. I think some of the derided scientists involved in seemingly bizarre research, like Albert Budden, are on the way to answers that will change our understanding of our own world and solve UFO cases. But I also think that a few cases are so baffling in the face of all our current understanding that we can't begin to explain them. These are some of my favourite cases, along with the really mad ones.

I've had my own UFO-related experiences, but I think them all explicable. By far the most memorable was the time that government agents chased my car up a Kent road with the intention of shooting me and my little boy dead. That day taught me a lot. The story is coming up later in the book.

Right now, it is time for a brief history of bafflement.

Historical Precedents

The modern era of UFO investigation and popular appeal started in 1947 but UFO events are almost as old as recorded time.

It is an article of faith amongst many UFO proponents that the ancient texts of several religions describe UFO events. This view is seldom shared by scholars of the religions in question. The claims of the UFO proponents revolve around the description of incredible events and their similarity to modern UFO reports. A further claim amongst the UFO fraternity is that the events described from a range of ancient texts describe the same phenomena. The conclusion drawn is that this consistency is clear evidence that involvement with UFOs and their occupants was a regular feature of the lives of ancient peoples.

Erich Von Daniken's multimillion selling *Chariots Of The Gods*[6] and a host of other successful titles have presented a world in which alien spacecraft regularly landed in ancient times. Within the UFO community itself opinions are divided as to the meaning, if any, of these events. The most ambitious claims posit a kind of galactic garden theory in which aliens engineered Earth's biological and social future. These claims include the belief amongst some that aliens invented our religions and created mankind. This is often linked to the assertion in the book of *Genesis* that God made Man in his own image. The 'God' in question being an alien scientist.

Such arguments have many detractors. Some say that the term alternative archaeologist is a fitting description for some of the field's best-known proponents since their main archaeological tools appear to be an armchair, a pile of books and an active imagination. Alternative archaeology/ancient astronaut investigators, like many proponents of UFO existence, are derided for their reliance on sloppy and unscientific reasoning, but the criticism of the sceptics is probably most cutting for historical investigators whose evidence relies on interpretation of historic events and revisions of scientific viewpoints.

In his demolition of UFOlogy, James Oberg pointed out that the 'residue fallacy' in which some unexplained data is used to support a claim is plain bad science. This is certainly true of the basics of the ancient astronaut belief. Basically, Oberg is saying that the evidence of one hard-to-explain event, like the destruction of the cities of Sodom and Gomorrah and the changing of Lot's wife into a pillar of salt, doesn't prove that aliens used atomic weaponry on our ancestors.

There are some gripping mysteries in ancient texts. The pillar in the sky that led the Israelites from Egypt in *Exodus* chapter 13 being one prime case. The Israelites were familiar with comets and stars, so the description of an airborne fire at night and airborne pillar of cloud by day may suggest some unique phenomena.

The descriptions of many key events in ancient texts are vivid and spectacular. It is possible to dismiss many UFO-related claims on this material as supposition but some substantial investigations retain their power. NASA scientist Josef F Blumrich laughed his way through most of *Chariots Of The Gods* and set out to mount a scientific assault on the one section of the book that presented serious evidence he could challenge, i.e. the section dealing with the experience of the prophet Ezekiel. Here Blumrich found some details he could develop. At the time Blumrich was chief of NASA's Advanced Structural Development Branch with a CV that included work on Saturn V rockets, satellites, Skylab and The Space Shuttle. He would go on to earn NASA's Exceptional Service Medal.

Working from Ezekiel's descriptions Blumrich discovered that he could develop technical drawings and specifications that resembled workable spacecraft. Having set out on a part-time quest to rubbish what he saw as fanciful claims Blumrich, like J Allen Hynek before him, found his scepticism overturned by the evidence. As he noted in the opening of *The Spaceships Of Ezekiel*[7], 'Hardly ever was a total defeat so rewarding, so fascinating, and so delightful!' Ezekiel's account is a riot of events: "A great whirlwind came out of the North… and a fire unfolding itself... out of the midst thereof came the likeness of four living creatures.' However, it was Ezekiel's description of airborne wheels within wheels that prompted Blumrich's work.

Ezekiel described a wheel but Blumrich analysed the performance characteristics and appearance in the description. It led to scale drawings, a model craft that performed superbly in a wind tunnel and equations that suggested that all parts of the package, from the likely rate of burn of the propellant to the additional weight of the requisite radiation shield, were constructed to specifications the leading space engineers of Blumrich's era would recognise.

Blumrich was not alone in providing scientific support for alleged UFO events in ancient texts. Soviet physicist Professor M Agrest is one of a number of scientists to have outlined the obvious comparisons between the destruction of Sodom and Gomorrah and an atomic explosion. In his view, Lot's wife was too close to the event and, far from salt, she was probably reduced to a well-incinerated pile of ashes. Astrophysicist Carl Sagan[8] had a high-profile career that included cutting-edge work for NASA and an abiding interest in the search for extraterrestrial life. Sagan had little truck with much popular UFOlogy, frequently acting as an erudite sceptic, but in 1966 he co-authored *Intelligent Life In The Universe*, a book openly speculating on extraterrestrial visitations of Earth in the distant past. This book and a number of others brought about a golden age of ancient astronaut writing in the 1960s and 1970s.[9] The quality of writing and research in the area, both then and now, is variable. Ultimately, it is the evidence that keeps this aspect of UFO interest alive. Some evidence, such as the Biblical account that spawned Josef Blumrich's book, is really a matter of faith. There is logic in the attempts to revisit fantastic historic accounts in the light of current technology but we can't prove that Ezekiel encountered space travellers any more than we can prove the Resurrection to an atheist.

Another strand of evidence is more tangible to modern science. A series of artefacts including the pyramids and ancient maps has continually fed the belief of extraterrestrial intervention in our history. The basis of the belief is that the production of such artefacts was beyond the technology available to ancient peoples. An enticing mystery surrounds a series of ancient maps. The best-known is Piri Re'is' portolan. A portolan is a practical map showing the route from port to port. Erich Von Daniken shows a projection of this ancient map and discusses its uncanny accuracy when plotted against a US Navy map from the 1960s. The staggering feature of the map is its detailed depiction of the east coast of South America and the coast of Antarctica. Piri Re'is was a

Turkish admiral in the days when such employment generally amounted to licensed piracy. The map was a copy of earlier maps, believed to have been in the possession of Christopher Columbus. Re'is' professional belligerence finally caught up with him. His final public appearance was a crowd-pleasing gorefest involving the forcible separation of his head from his body in 1554. Officially, the coast of Antarctica was discovered in 1818.

Von Daniken wasn't alone in finding significance in this map. The US Navy were intrigued after studying it and noted from a 1949 survey that it accurately depicted land under the polar ice cap. This is land covered by ice for at least 2,000 years and probably more than twice that time. Donald Keyhoe, a retired US Marine Corps Major, detailed a discussion with Captain John Brent, a military training school buddy. In *Flying Saucers—Top Secret*, Keyhoe quotes Brent saying that the Piri Re'is map, "Is so accurate only one thing could explain it... a worldwide aerial survey." This survey would have to pre-date the last ice age.

The bold "only one thing could explain it" assertion typifies many of the claims in ancient astronaut/alternative archaeology writing. It is also demonstrably wrong. Professor of Anthropology Charles Hapgood was also aware of Re'is' map and many other intriguing portolans. His own research, outlined in *Earth's Shifting Crust* (1959) and *Maps Of The Ancient Sea Kings* (1966), suggested the possibility that rapid shifts in the Earth's crust had moved continents thousands of miles, wiping out much evidence of civilisation and leaving a few fragments, like the accurate maps, with the survivors. Hapgood's theory fits wider legends of lost civilisations as well as most of the ancient astronaut beliefs. Ultimately much of the evidence for ancient astronauts is a puzzling jumble that makes fleeting sense when woven into a legend that allows the brilliant skill of super-intelligent aliens to fill in the gaps. These stories may be true but, to date, all we've proven beyond doubt is the existence of the mysteries.

One of the most intriguing stories is covered in *The Sirius Mystery*, a work first published in 1976.[10] Oddly, the author Robert Temple was concerned that his best-selling book should be considered in the same breath as works like *Chariots Of The Gods*. Temple's work concentrates on the Dogon tribe of Mali and a belief in their culture that fish-like beings, called the Nommos, had visited Earth in the past. Temple's assured study links folk beliefs in both Africa and the Middle East, and establishes legends amongst the Dogon that include detailed knowledge of astronomy and physics which appear to have beaten modern science to key discoveries. Notably the knowledge that the star Sirius has a heavy companion orbiting the main star once every fifty years. If, as many assert, this is folk belief handed down over thousands of years, then it pre-dates the discovery of Sirius B and the subsequent discovery that it was a super-heavy White Dwarf star. The accuracy of much Dogon knowledge is beyond question and the difference between their own folk legends and those of most other African tribes also lends weight to this ancient astronaut theory. It is possible, but highly unlikely, that passing missionaries taught the tribe. The Dogon tribe are convinced that there is a third star, Sirius C. Science requires more than the tradition of an African tribe before claiming a discovery. A few claims were made about its discovery in the 1920s. Since then it has not been seen again. If the star or its remains are ever discovered, remember where you read it first.

These stories are a representative handful in an area of investigation that posits a range of alternative cosmologies and histories of our planet. Much of the alternative archaeology movement concerns itself with reinterpreting past societies and a good deal of this work owes nothing to UFO investigations and ideas. At the other extreme there are ideas and investigations of mind-numbing complexity. Ancient astronaut theories have some strange relatives. Some investigators firmly believe that alien visitations are the result of highly evolved beings from our own history maintaining their contact with Earth. The survivors of Atlantis are a predictable addition to this debate but they are not alone. British UFOlogist David Barclay is one of a number of researchers who believe that dinosaurs evolved into the well-known grey aliens of the present.[11]

The publishing explosion that followed *Chariots Of The Gods* continues but, as with most areas of the UFO debate, the Internet is now the real home of unfettered coverage of the UFO mysteries of the ancient past. If this opening section has you itching to surf the net, a visit to a detailed site, like that offered by Grace Watcher, could be the start of a lengthy period of missing time for you.[12]

Fairies, Flaps And Fundamentals

Recorded history over the last 2,000 years shows us how everything we know as normal everyday life evolved. It also suggests that UFO events, in all their varied forms, have been a constant throughout this time.

This section will be slightly different to the last. We have a reasonable historical record of who did what to whom, so this cuts down on the more extreme speculations. Instead, we get UFO events taking place and a number of differing opinions struggling to make sense of them. There are thousands of sightings recorded over the last 20 centuries or so: lights in the sky; abduction experiences; the utterly incomprehensible; and the occasional hoax. Making sense of the stories at this distance and with no physical evidence is impossible. Using them to inform our current understanding is a little more useful. The past lacks photographic and radar evidence but that is about the only significant difference.

There is no shortage of images. Pictures from China and Persia show airborne craft looking for all the world like small boxes with people inside them. Strange astral events find their way into a series of pictures, often showing unfortunate earthlings throwing back their heads and gesturing at the sky. Probably the most famous image of this time records the appearance of black and white globes over Basle in Switzerland in 1566. It shows a sky crowded with UFOlogy's answer to Piccadilly Circus whilst a stunned group of onlookers show that overacting was a problem long before cheap Hollywood B-films. Elsewhere, the technology of the day clearly affected the way people represented the reports. An etching currently in the possession of the New York Public Library shows aerial ships over France. We are talking ships with sails and rigging, with the predictable stunned onlookers on the ground. One witness in a small rowing boat is also, unwisely, standing and reacting theatrically.

Then as now, people read significance into such events. On a number of occasions royal proclamations or parliamentary time somewhere around the world resulted from UFO reports. The Emperor Charlemagne once outlawed aerial travel. The event which prompted this involved four people seen coming to land near Lyons in France from a strange aerial vehicle. The bemused locals suspected that the people were sorcerers sent by an enemy to destroy crops. The locals were taken against their will and shown incredible things. The visitors were outnumbered and, facing a hostile mob, the situation was heading for the predictable "we don't trust you so we'll build a bonfire" finale when Agobard, the respected local Archbishop, intervened. Agobard had seen none of the events but pointed out that they couldn't have happened and, therefore, the bemused strangers and raging locals had obviously been wrong. The strangers were set free and the event went into history.

Such stories have echoes in current events in which researchers and witnesses struggle to agree with expert explanations for cases given by people who were never there. Similarly, those closer to the cases often have well-established suspicions that colour their experience whilst the witnesses display confusion.

Distant historical accounts contain their rarities. Octagons have never been common in UFO reports but one such object was observed on 15 April 1752 near Stavanger in Norway. They also show a gradual move toward the patterns of today. By the end of the nineteenth century UFO flaps were also becoming common. 'Flap' is another loose UFOlogical term, generally used to describe a profusion of events that centre themselves at a particular time and place. There is no agreed number of reports or any definite time period applied to a flap.

A rash of reports from Wales at the start of the last century represents an early British flap. A brilliant disc over the principality on 1 February 1905 was followed by an intensely dark object over Llangollen on 2 September. On 18 May 1909 a Cardiff man walking near Caerphilly reported an event that would find close parallels with many later reports. He encountered a large cylindrical object next to a road. Two odd looking men in fur coats were inside, clearly speaking some strange foreign language. As the man approached, the object took off and headed away at great speed.

This final report bears some similarity to a rash of 'phantom airship' sightings that plagued the USA between 1896 and 1897. At the time it was widely believed that at least one brilliant inventor was at work on a craft that would revolutionise air transport. However, there is virtually no chance that such a vehicle was remotely close to a prototype. The vivid reports that became a regular feature of the papers pushed new boundaries in detail and helped to establish several staple items in UFO reports. In one case a railroad conductor, James Hooten, claimed to have come upon a landed airship. He described "wheels" with blades driven by jets of air blown onto them. The captain of the ship had a brief conversation with Hooten during which he explained that the ship used "compressed air and aeroplanes." If this sounds familiar then remember that the best-selling fiction of Jules Verne was written around this time.

The airship legends continue as a substantial part of most detailed histories of the subject although it is almost certain that the major stories that drive this area of accounts are hoaxes. An animal abduction and mutilation story in which a rancher finds an airship hovering over his cattle, before plucking one on a thin line and leaving it decimated, was concocted by rancher Alexander Hamilton. The most famous case of the whole flap involved a crash retrieval, including the body of the pilot at Aurora, Texas, on 17 April 1897. The *Dallas Morning News* report stated of the pilot: 'while his remains are badly disfigured, enough of the original has been picked up to show that he was not an inhabitant of this world.' The ship also, apparently, contained writing in 'unknown hieroglyphics.'

Since the flap of 1896/7 the stories have circulated widely, appearing in various guises in the UFO literature and being discussed in terms of their importance to the modern day. It is beyond dispute that we have templates we would easily recognise in modern stories. James Hooten's encounter is typical of many, before and after, in which some aspect of technology just ahead of that known to humanity at the time was confidently demonstrated by a UFO occupant. Cattle mutilations continue to be reported to this day, many showing a clear resemblance to Alexander Hamilton's hoaxed claim. In other famous crash retrieval stories we find claims of strange hieroglyphic writing on debris from the wrecked UFO.

Extensive writing has been done on the US airship flap but the few who have checked the original sources have found clear evidence of hoaxing. Alexander Hamilton was a member of a serious-liars club, whilst there seems little evidence that anyone around Aurora, Texas, ever took the crash retrieval seriously. Recently the story has represented a local nuisance as UFOlogists push to open graves and exhume the remains of the dead pilot. British folklorist and UFO researcher David Clarke produced a succinct dismissal of the whole hysterical episode as the opening chapter of a co-authored work *The UFOs That Never Were*.[13] The odd aspect from this distance is the way that admitted hoaxes from the late nineteenth century bear an uncanny resemblance to apparently sincere reports in the present day.

Nowhere is this more marked than in the overlap between reports of meetings with creatures from alternative realities, like fairies and nature spirits, and present-day abduction reports. This whole aspect of UFO investigation has produced a copious and contradictory literature. Crudely, researchers chase two lines of argument. A literal approach claims reports of meetings with goblins, fairies and their ilk as the product of meetings between our simple-minded ancestors and aliens. A more involved argument forms part of the so-called 'new UFOlogy.' This is a branch of investigation taking a broad view and allowing ideas from mysticism, folklore and psychology. These ideas are used to look at UFO events as potential evidence of a range of phenomena including the convergence of one or more dimensions of existence. Less literal than the nuts-and-bolts investigations, new UFOlogy can claim one of two fathers, Carl Jung or Jacques Vallee. Vallee concerns us here because his early works[14] broke new ground in opening up investigations of present-day UFO cases in conjunction with established traditions of folk belief. The case outlined earlier from Lyons appears in *Passport To Magonia* (1969 France, 1970 UK) alongside long discussions on the uncanny link between stories of encounters with beings from the fairy realms.

It is easy to overlook the fact that for most of the last 5,000 years so-called superstitious beliefs have been part of everyday reality for many people around the world. It is only in the recent past that they have been relegated by rationality to the fringes of our lives. This relegation has, in any case, struggled to succeed. Belief in the power of astrology, the reality of angels and the presence of spiritual entities within nature remains stronger than many people realise. The lore surrounding such beliefs has built up over centuries. When Jacques Vallee started on his ground-breaking study he drew on major works like Walter Evans Wetz's *The Fairy Kingdom In Celtic Countries, Its Psychological Origin And Nature*. Wetz's book, published in 1909, presented a world in which a contradictory collection of beings, from mischievous elves to the well-meaning fairies, interfered in the lives of ordinary people. The people targeted were often unable to describe their experiences accurately and those in the position of listening to such descriptions were left struggling to believe the accounts. Many items which would subsequently become staples of UFO cases consistently appear in tales of the fairy kingdom. Many attempts to remove items from the fairy kingdom as proof of a visit appear to come to grief. The beings from the kingdom seem able to shape-shift and often appear in unfamiliar and confusing disguises. Time spent in the realm of these elemental beings may pass at a different rate to time for those left behind. In one case from Wales a man missing for three weeks believed he had only been gone for three hours. Messages gathered from the fairy kingdom may be contradictory and predictions have a tendency to amount to nothing but, despite the problems, there is a peculiar consistency. The people contacted are often left clinging to stories which do them no favours in terms of their credibility. One of my favourite UFO cases of all time started its high-profile life in the writing of Jacques Vallee. Many of the nuts-and-bolts UFO crowd don't rate the bizarre case of Joe Simonton and his pancakes at all.[15]

Simonton, a chicken farmer from Eagle River, Wisconsin, spent a strange few minutes on 18 April 1961 doing the bidding of a trio of small men inside a shiny craft. He gave them water, they gave him some rough and tasteless pancakes, one of which was later analysed by the Food and Drug Laboratory of the US Department of Health, Education and Welfare. The analysis, carried out at the behest of the US Air Force, found the pancakes to be quite ordinary and 'of terrestrial origin.' Support for Simonton came from J Allen Hynek who was called to investigate that case and concluded, 'There is no question that Mr Simonton felt that his contact had been a real experience.' Simonton's case corresponds with reported fairy lore in which food loses its flavour and all sense of life when passed from the fairy realm to our world. His sincere account of an experience that belongs in a third-rate sci-fi novel is also another regular feature of fairy lore.

Had Simonton's encounter happened a century earlier he would doubtless be regarded as, quite literally, telling a fairy story. His case belongs instead in the 'High Strangeness' files of the modern UFO era, an era we must now visit.

This section has demonstrated that much of what we will find there may have roots that stretch back centuries. The present age, the age when 'Flying Saucer' and 'UFO' became dictionary entries and labels likely to generate income, started on 24 June 1947.

Okay Ken, Open Those Floodgates

On 24 June 1947 Kenneth Arnold was flying his Callair aircraft near Mount Rainier in Washington State. He joined the search for a missing C-46 transport plane. He didn't find it. The wreckage and bodies would turn up soon enough and make a fleeting news item. Arnold, by contrast, would be credited with starting a phenomenon.

Arnold sighted nine objects flying in formation. Startled at the way the sun glinted off the objects and their rapid movement he began to take crude measurements. He estimated their speed at between 1,300 and 1,700 miles an hour, easily in excess of the fastest aircraft of the time. Using another aircraft in the sky, a DC-4 at some distance, Arnold managed to make some estimates of the size of the objects and length of the formation. He believed the objects to be two thirds the size of the DC-4 and estimated the formation to be spread over five miles of sky. Arnold's initial reaction was to believe the objects were military hardware, possibly missiles, under test. He radioed his sighting ahead and discussed what he had seen with fellow pilots after landing at Pendleton, Oregon. Within hours the news wires were starting to buzz with the story that heralded the era of the flying saucer.

Arnold's sighting is unremarkable in the context of the mind-numbing conspiracy claims that stalk the current literature. His conviction regarding guided missiles came from his initial discussions with other pilots. He would soon be persuaded towards an alien interpretation. The explosion of publicity that greeted the case unleashed a hysteria that would resolutely refuse to go back in the box. In retrospect, Kenneth Arnold's sighting is the perfect case to open the era of UFOs as a popular interest. Apart from anything else, the case has something for everyone: a vivid image on which to hang the whole story; odd twists; incredible speculation; and an unsung hero.

The claims made by Arnold were repeated around the world. Arnold became a celebrity and remained a figure of some veneration in the UFO world until his death in 1984. The dissection of the case by the media soon established that nothing man-made could achieve the reported speed of Arnold's objects. Within weeks further reports were coming in. Arnold himself fielded a fusillade of phone calls and letters, many reporting similar sightings and a substantial proportion firmly in the "Thank God, at last somebody understands me" camp. The image of the little plane sharing the sky with a saucer squadron was sensational and allowed room for public speculation. There was no obvious conventional explanation. Given the scale of other reports and the lack of any obvious new military hardware matching the incredible performance of Arnold's flying saucers, the common consent was that Kenneth Arnold had seen alien spacecraft.

Nothing pushed the cause of this case more than the term 'flying saucers.' The term and explosion of saucer popularity is one insight into the way truth and apparent truth develop in UFO cases. Kenneth Arnold described crescent- or boomerang-shaped objects. The term saucer came from his comment that the objects moved "like a saucer would if you skipped it across water." Bill Becquette, a reporter for the *East Oregonian*, heard the description and coined the term flying saucer. Whatever the accuracy of his report, Becquette remains one of the UFO world's unsung heroes. Without his crowd-pleasing summation of the incident we would have been denied a phrase that would popularise the whole business of sighting unusual airborne objects.

Nobody was with Arnold in his plane but interpretations of his experience had already distorted the truth. Within days the popular image of flying saucers and discs became the norm in other reports. The first instance of the word saucer being used in relation to UFO cases goes back to the American airship flap of the previous century and, as it had exactly fifty years before, the news industry once more made money on the back of UFO reports. Arnold's efforts to measure speed, size and distance gave the report an air of authority. But nobody else was there and his credibility has been called into question as succeeding generations of investigators have sought to put their own spin on the story. Alien spacecraft remains the popular option, especially in the stream of big-selling books that take the angle that aliens are regular visitors and/or in league with at least one government on Earth.

Several commentators have highlighted the contradiction between Arnold's report of crescent- or wing-shaped objects and the later popular acceptance of saucer-shaped craft. A photograph exists of him holding a drawing showing the shape of the objects. Arnold would go on to write an article stating 'I did see the discs' and a book called *The Coming Of The Saucers* (1952). Amongst others, David Barclay goes as far as to suggest that Arnold was a covert intelligence operative involved in trying to bring the whole idea of UFOs into ridicule.[16] By comparison

James Easton's detailed analysis in *Fortean Times* gathers the information into a well-referenced argument suggesting that Arnold simply made a mistake when spotting a flight of white pelicans.[17] Predictably this claim went down like a lead brick in cyberspace and public houses frequented by people who believe firmly in an alien presence on this planet. At first glance Easton's claim appears to be the UFOlogical equivalent of discovering the lost handwritten note in Marx's original *Das Kapital* manuscript reading, 'This crap is gonna make me rich!' It disturbed some of the alien conspiracy crowd all the more because, on close inspection, Easton's analysis is logical, researched to exemplary standards and supported by solid evidence. It doesn't rate high in the crowd-pleasing stakes, but it may well explain the events of 24 June 1947.

Easton's argument is specific to the Arnold case but we should note that speculation on life in outer space and the potential for alien visits was well advanced in 1947. In one notable event Dr Layman Spitzer Jr., associate professor of astrophysics at Yale University, speculated on radio that Martians may have already visited Earth. The day after the programme a national US newspaper ran a report on his ideas. This matters because the dates of radio show and newspaper report are 22 and 23 June 1947, two days before Kenneth Arnold's sighting![18]

But just when it looks like a climate of mass awareness of possible alien life could have caused hysteria in Arnold and his audience this case, like so many others, throws us a curve. A prospector on the ground at the time reported a sighting that appeared to support Arnold's report. The prospector's sighting lasted around a minute, allowing him time to use a telescope and focus on one 'disc' in a formation of similar objects.[19] This confuses the issue but we can be sure that the popular image of Arnold encountering classic flying saucer-shaped discs is a myth. Another certainty is that the case made Arnold a more reflective and cynical human being. "Believe me," he said, "If I ever see again a phenomenon of that sort in the sky, even if it's a one-story building, I won't say a word about it!"[20]

So the modern era had begun. Since 1947 airborne objects have been a mainstay of UFO investigation. Such reports these days draw little excitement from some seasoned investigators. In the wake of Kenneth Arnold there have been spectacular cases, incredible claims and several precedents firmly set. The following chapters will deal with several of these events like, for example, the events at Roswell, New Mexico. They occurred within a fortnight of Kenneth Arnold's sighting but caused little stir at the time following a US Army Air Force press conference explaining the initial 'crashed disc' report as a mis-identified weather balloon.

Within five years of the Arnold sighting two new features to UFO cases were well established: overflights of huge numbers of objects; and radar-visual sightings. One brief flap contained both. On the night of 19/20 July 1952 Washington was buzzed by at least eight unidentified objects which flew into restricted airspace over The White House and made themselves scarce as jet fighters belatedly arrived. Exactly a week later a repeat performance was staged with more targets and, briefly, an air force fighter apparently surrounded in mid-air as the frightened pilot radioed for instructions. The publicity was huge and the official explanation, that the pilots and radar personnel had simply mis-identified the effects of temperature inversions, impressed no one.

This case boasts witnesses on the ground, radar operators convinced they were dealing with real targets, military pilots unable to push their machines to match the airborne objects and civilian pilots diverted to see the same objects. Radar tracks suggested speeds of up to 7,000 mph, a performance beyond the best military aircraft today. There is also clear evidence that Captain Edward J Ruppelt, then in charge of an official US investigation into UFOs, was actively misled and hindered during the events.[21] On the face of it this case is a classic. It remains unexplained and some of the evidence, like the reported speeds of the objects, suggests no conventional explanation is possible.

Predictably, there is some scepticism. More importantly, the Washington overflights introduce other elements of UFO lore that are now an accepted part of the whole business. Namely, the conspiracy and cover-up angles. It is a standard belief amongst many that the US government has knowledge of UFOs, and has possibly agreed with those operating the craft to trade their technology in exchange for non-interference in the abduction of US citizens. The Washington case has echoes of conspiracy. Edward J Ruppelt was warned that a major UFO event was likely to happen before the Washington case. At the time he was head of Project Blue Book, an official US government investigation into UFOs, and yet he was hindered in investigating the case. The implication is obvious and is supported by many events and much evidence since 1952. There is a level of secrecy above those officially acknowledged to exist and some UFO investigation is handled at this level.

Clear evidence of cover-up does not prove the existence of aliens. Some research links the sensational UFO stories of the 1950s with the US government's attempt to use the hysteria to recruit the general public as both official and unofficial sky watchers. The cold war was escalating and there were serious gaps in America's fledgling radar coverage. If this is true, it was an inspired move.

The Washington case is, arguably, the first in another strand of UFO cases, the 'Holy Grail' report, which presents what appears to be the perfect case. Recent examples include the alleged crash of a gunned-down UFO in Botswana, the 'Manhattan Transfer' case in which a woman was reportedly floated out of a New York skyscraper in full view of the Secretary General of the United Nations, and the film of a supposed autopsy on a dead alien. The general trend amongst such cases is a spectacular launch on the world, a period of controversy and the eventual acceptance by most interested parties that the whole thing is a hoax. Of all the seemingly perfect cases the Washington overflights are the hardest to break. If they are genuine as written then they support the notion that the US government cut a deal after the UFOnauts demonstrated their superior power.

Other evidence includes: the odd feature of the two Saturday nights; the coincidence that on the first night the nearest military air base was inoperative because of runway repairs; the perfection of the case as a media feeding frenzy; and the apparent prior knowledge of a select few suggests a covert but earthbound operation. If so, this would be in a great military tradition. For example, the Stealth Bomber was tested against civilian radar. When it vanished within one sweep of a radar beam, generating UFO reports, the military knew the technology could work against an enemy.

But if the 1952 Washington flap was a covert operation it was one hell of a stunt. Despite so many people being involved, there have been no major leak of information to this day. Also, some of America's best radar facilities, both civilian and military, were fooled by returns moving at incredible speeds.

Less credible, but much more fun, are the 1950s contactees, a bizarre and colourful bunch who claimed direct contact with aliens. Most of the contactees appeared to meet B-movie characters who combined a surprisingly human appearance with a generally benevolent line in anti-nuclear rhetoric. George Adamski remains the most celebrated of this crowd. His monster-selling work *Flying Saucers Have Landed* (1953) details his meeting with a man from Venus. Adamski's celebrity led him, apparently, to a papal meeting. It also led to further books and a die-hard following, loyal to this day. If Adamski achieved the greatest market share, the most significant developments linked to contactees are probably those that took George King from a London taxi driver to a multi-titled religious leader preaching a complex cosmology. King claimed a 1958 contact on Holdstone Down in Devon and gathered a band of followers who continue to thrive after his death. Many in the UFO fraternity mock the beliefs of The Aetherius Society and, at face value, they do seem incredible. They say that all the planets in our solar system are inhabited, mainly by beings who exist in realities beyond the detection of our science. Jesus is alive and well and was the being who met King in 1958. King was subsequently involved in inter-planetary conflict and helped to save our planet. Chanting Buddhist mantras en masse can charge prayer power batteries which can subsequently beam their energies to prevent conflict and disaster. Ridiculous or not, King's Aetherian followers maintain their headquarters in Fulham, present a media-friendly face to the world and are obviously happier and more ful-filled for their involvement. The foundations of the group may see them compared to other more dangerous cults but, in my journalistic experi-ence at least, The Aetherius Society are probably the most helpful and sincere UFO-related organisation I have ever approached. And, before you ask, I don't buy their belief system.

Truman Bethurum's book *Aboard A Flying Saucer* (1954) is a con-noisseur's contactee. His romance with Aura Rhanes, who is "tops for shapeliness and beauty," is classic pulp science fiction, but it is pre-sented as fact. As is *Flying Saucer From Mars*, the account of a 1954 meeting between the mysterious Cedric Allingham and a Martian on a Scottish beach. Complete with blurry photographs of the Martian and his ship, the book reads like a blatant parody of Adamski's best-selling story. The book retains an interest amongst the UFO community where it is widely believed that television astronomer Patrick Moore was involved in its creation as either an amusing little earner or a deliberate attempt to prove the credulity of the flying saucer fan base.[22]

From the end of the 1950s more serious contacts were being reported. It is debatable when the era of the abductee began. In recent years many abduction reports have been collected and every strange disappearance, from the Lighthousemen of the Flannan Isles to Moses' gathering of the ten commandments, has been claimed as an abduction by someone.

In 1958 Antonio Villas Boas claimed an abduction from a farm in Brazil. His story involved coerced sex with an alien female who indicated through gestures that she would have his baby. In 1964 an American couple, Barney and Betty Hill, were chased in their car by a bright light, experienced missing time and subsequent nightmares, and eventually underwent hypnosis. At this stage of the investigation memories of an abduction experience were unearthed. The therapist involved, Dr Benjamin Simon, was asked if he thought the memories were real and replied "absolutely not."[23] However, there is evidence that the object the Hills saw was tracked on radar.[24] The Hill's case became public knowledge before the Brazilian event and is, therefore, arguably the first modern abduction. Either way, by the mid-1960s there were complex and sometimes contradictory reports of human beings being taken out of their environment by aliens who appeared to have a distinct interest in our reproductive capabilities. Then the debate began about whether this was happening in the minds of the witnesses or in reality. The complex argument, which is fuelled by many more investigations, still rages and we'll see more in chapter three.

The concept of UFOs covers everything from the more vivid parts of *The Bible* to the possibility that aliens are already amongst us. The experts don't agree about any of it. We lack definitive answers because UFOlogy is an investigation that still needs to find itself. One of these days we might be smart enough to ask the right questions.

2. The Evidence For Alien Invaders

UFO investigators do not study UFOs. They study reports. The best reports make the kind of cases we have already begun to outline. They lead people to believe in particular explanations. In most cases this belief is a matter of faith. The faith runs deep. Differing opinions have been known to result in the hurling of both insults and writs on a regular basis. Arguably, this has deprived UFOlogy of the kind of wide-ranging investigations that would genuinely shake out answers. One effect of this infighting is that sceptics are convinced that there is nothing to investigate.

When I'm not writing for a living I work in Dartford, teaching others to write for a living. In a college that offers a range of Higher Education you would expect some enlightened thinking. But a week before writing these words I was talking to one colleague, discussing my latest writing projects. "Oh neat," she said, "They pay you to write a book on something that doesn't exist."

"Have you ever seen anything you couldn't explain in the sky?" I asked.

"Well... yes, but..."

"But what?"

"There's no evidence is there?"

Wrong! There is plenty of evidence. The problems start when we ask the next question. Evidence for what?

The 'no evidence' belief generally comes attached to another thought, that UFOs mean aliens. There is no hard, incontestable proof of alien existence. There is much faith that such proof exists and many people think this proof is in the hands of the US government. The evidence for this belief remains the most lucrative material in the UFO world and best-selling books like Timothy Good's *Above Top Secret* (1987) and *Beyond Top Secret* (1996)[1] build cases into an argument claiming that a range of hard-to-explain events lead us to one conclusion, i.e. the existence of aliens has been covered up.

The problem with this argument is that proving alien existence is extremely hard. This is true in both the popular and scientific domain. In scientific terms it borders on trying to prove a negative, i.e. that something did not originate on Earth. The book in your hands now could have originated on another planet[2] assuming they had paper, inks and the requisite chemicals. Scientifically you could only prove the make-up of the constituent parts and use other information like the publisher's address to trace its origin. All of which might constitute acceptable proof in a court of law. But it could still be fabricated. In which case the evidence you needed for alien existence could be in your hands and disguised as something else.

There are those who would claim there is hard evidence of alien existence that is misunderstood in a similar fashion. If you have best-selling books like those mentioned, access to the Internet and key terms like 'Area 51,' 'Implant' and 'Men in Black' and a spare six months you may investigate these ideas in real depth. You will, however, not come across hard definitive proof that would convince a non-believer.

So, at risk of offending those who believe in the proven existence of aliens and also at risk of disappointing those of you who want the spectacular secrets in return for your £3.99, I'd like to suggest another route through the evidence. Look at the different threads, consider what we know for sure and wonder where it might lead us. If that is a disappointment please remember what I said in the introduction, that this is a subject in which an amateur investigator can still strive to make the most incredible discoveries and the most active mind can find a lifetime of lateral thinking. If you want discoveries that will shake the world you could do worse than study what you'll find in this chapter and get involved yourself.

Hard evidence comes in many different forms. Physical objects, mysterious traces, useable data for social scientific investigation and, occasionally, the truly inexplicable.

The Hard Stuff

The really hard evidence is the things you can see, feel and hold. There is no shortage of claims relating to such evidence. One area of belief suggests that we have all, indirectly, handled such hard evidence. For my money *Men In Black* is one of the best UFO movies ever made, not least because of its solid roots in UFO lore. At one point a stunned Will Smith asks how the incredible space port is funded. Tommy Lee Jones casually explains that a rake off from back-engineered alien technology ("microwave ovens, Velcro, computers") is sufficient. One strand of UFO belief claims that back-engineering is there for all to see. Back-engineering is a term you won't find in a standard dictionary. Like many UFO-related phrases it has a loose meaning, crudely equating to stripping down advanced technology, understanding it and recreating it to meet our own needs.

Forget the microwave ovens for a second. UFO-related tourism is an under-appreciated feature of the present world. Just ask my wife where we spent our honeymoon! One hot spot is Area 51, Groom Lake, Nevada. A lonely expanse of dusty desert and dry mountains to which a dedicated band have laid siege for several years. The result has been fleeting glimpses of airborne lights performing manoeuvres which appear beyond the capabilities of all known aircraft. The videos and photographs have been widely reproduced and all shades of UFO opinion would probably agree on some of the main points about Groom Lake.

a) The base is the site of testing for future generations of US military hardware.

b) Security personnel and restricted access to certain areas are there to protect the secrets under development.

c) The objects observed and videotaped are hard, physical evidence supporting the above statements.

To the people seeing and interpreting these sights the objects are UFOs. Literally, unidentified and flying. UFO literature, Websites and conferences drown in claims that this site is where alien technology is back-engineered. A number of people, notably Americans Bob Oechsler and Bob Lazar, have come forward to claim direct involvement in these projects. Lazar's claims include his involvement in attempting to replicate an alien propulsion system with terrestrial materials. Lazar claimed the system was based on an antimatter reactor. Despite official denials of his involvement Lazar has been able to produce some hard evidence of his own in the form of a payslip and internal phone directory to indicate he was inside the facility.[3]

This only proves that the area is sensitive. But, despite government denials, we already knew that. Opened in 1954, the base has been home to secret projects like the Lockheed SR-71 Blackbird, the U-2 spyplane and the B-2 Stealth Bomber. To date, the hard evidence proves only that the technology on site starts somewhere around the cutting edge and aims for a realm way beyond that. Exciting for sure but the evidence of alien involvement still rests on the reports and reputations of those who claim to know.

The alleged alien implants don't look anywhere near as exciting as a B-2 Stealth Bomber but they have fallen into the hands of ordinary UFOlogists and rank and file laboratories. Implant lore is complicated. The crude claim is that one feature of abductions is the forcible insertion of small objects into those abducted. Evidence for implants includes x-ray images and supporting medical testimony. For example, a common location for implants in humans is in the upper reaches of the nose. Some of those allegedly implanted have reported spontaneous nose-bleeds. The claimed purpose of the implants involves monitoring physical and emotional reactions and tracking the abductee. The ways in which these small and varied objects achieve this aim is harder to establish.

A few alleged implants have been surgically removed. The retrieved objects have been examined with predictably ambiguous results. The parting shot in a statement from one investigator provides the perfect summation to the problem. In his best-selling *Abduction* Harvard psychiatrist John E Mack discusses the analysis undertaken on an implant retrieved from the nose of a young woman. An analysis of the elements it contained proved the presence of elements including carbon, silicon and oxygen. A nuclear biologist told Mack that the item was not a biological specimen but "could be a manufactured fibre." As Mack succinctly states, "It seemed difficult to know how to proceed further."[4]

Difficult for several reasons. Firstly there was no proven alien artefact with which to compare the implant. Secondly, the implant was an anomalous collection of elements, making any kind of positive identification a matter of luck and guesswork at best. Most implants end their short stint under the microscope in this way. They are identified only in terms of their make-up. Their real purpose and origin are a matter of conjecture.

In favour of the notion that this hard evidence amounts to alien intervention are several circumstantial points. There is some consistency in the location of implants, the upper reaches of the nose being a particular favourite. Time and again the implants are impossible to trace to any specific earthly origin. They could be a manufactured fibre. But whose manufactured fibre? A number of medical professionals have been willing to stand up and support the belief in implants. Dr Roger Lier has allowed cameras into the operating theatre as he removed alleged implants. This process proves that some of the objects in question are genuinely retrieved from inside human bodies.

The hard evidence can be read differently. Since the objects appear to be made of elements found readily on Earth it is entirely possible that many, if not all, are accidentally taken into the skin and remain there harmlessly. The 'Strange Days' section of *Fortean Times* magazine runs many medical curiosity stories, some of which involve people who have remained blissfully unaware of objects as large as nails in their bodies for years. There is also a clear possibility of fraud in some cases. The things that people will do to themselves and their bodies push the bounds of believability. One doctor in Israel has an astonishing collection of objects removed from the rear ends of his fellow human beings whilst *Fortean Times* editor Bob Rickard once told me a story about a man who repeatedly swallowed a boiled doll's head. This was the same head, swallowed, passed and boiled time after time. There is a difference in motive between the auto-erotic creativity of these fun lovers and the alleged implant victims. But, the point remains, that some people do things to their bodies that the rest of us would never contemplate. In such company, those wilfully deceiving themselves and others about the origin of a strange sliver of metal under their skin may be some of the milder cases.

In addition to the implants there have been laboratory tests carried out on alleged debris from crashed craft. The belief in crash retrievals is a major part of many general UFO tomes. The stories are generally set against a wider scenario in which governments gather information about the true purpose of alien races through the accidental acquisition of craft and their occupants. Most of the evidence for such stories begins and ends, like the case of Bob Lazar, with tantalising claims and secondary evidence in the form of drawings. A selection of items of dubious authenticity have been advanced over the years as claimed fragments of extraterrestrial craft. As with splinters of the true cross and other religious relics, the main reason to doubt such items is their somewhat contradictory nature. The alleged fragments of the craft that crashed at Roswell do not resemble each other and conspicuously lack the qualities claimed by some who state they handled the wreckage at the time.

There are some fragmentary clues to alien incursions into our airspace that are impossible to refute. Perhaps the best comes from a case dubbed 'The Siberian Spacefall' by Jenny Randles.[5] A burning aerial object stunned the scattered population of Siberia on 30 June 1908 before detonating over a remote forest area. Of all the reported UFO retrieval cases this one event has generated by far the greatest amount of hard physical evidence. On the day of the incident the fireball and heatwave that followed the explosion were experienced miles from the impact. A shock wave circled the Earth twice and damage to property extended almost 400 miles from the impact. By 1945 some of the scientific establishment noticed the clear similarity between photographs of the aftermaths of Tunguska and the American nuclear weaponry unleashed on Japan. At the start of the following year A Kasantsev, a Russian author, was first into print with an idea that is still attached to this case. In a short story he suggested that an alien spacecraft powered by nuclear engines had exploded over Siberia.

The hardest of all the hard evidence in this case is the presence of tiny debris embedded deep into tree stumps after the blast. These debris resemble fragments, called tektites, which result from the fusing of sand and rock during the intense heat of a nuclear blast. It is possible that a comet or meteorite caused the Tunguska event but no theory supporting either culprit provides a neat fit with the evidence. The most reliable theories suggest an airburst for the object around 3 miles above the ground. Eyewitness reports consistently state that the sound of the object was heard at the same time as it passed overhead. If so, it was moving below the speed of sound. Slower than a meteor or comet. The Siberian Spacefall is a classic UFO mystery. This is an undisputed event that is likely to celebrate its centenary without yielding to any attempt to explain it. As Jenny Randles says, "The debate rages on."

Tantalising Traces

Aside from the hard evidence, the most commonly advanced definitive proof for the existence of UFOs or aliens is that which leaves some kind of trace. Photographs, films and videos make the most spectacular evidence of this kind. The most convincing cases in this section are those which involve radar and evidence on the ground.

Photographic evidence could prove the case for extraterrestrial existence beyond doubt if the photographs themselves could be proven genuine. From the clear pictures of George Adamski to the dismemberment of the alien under autopsy in the infamous film first screened in the

1990s, this evidence has started its public career spectacularly and quickly found itself reduced to a hard core of supporters. The features that link much of this evidence are the murky origins of the material and inability of the owners to clear up the mess.

A handful of UFO photographs and films continue to defy all easy explanations and show little or no evidence of being hoaxes. Foremost amongst this collection is, arguably, a series of photographs taken by Brazilian photographer Almiro Barauna off Trinidade Island (not Trinidad as sometimes reported). On 16 January 1958 a Brazilian Navy ship was moored off the island when a saucer-shaped object circled the sharp peak and sped out to sea. Barauna's famous pictures show the object tilted at an angle. Blow-ups of the shots show a grainy texture to the object, which was witnessed by around fifty sailors. The texture of the images has led some, including British investigator Steuart Campbell, to suggest the image shows some unknown atmospheric phenomenon. It is possible, but disputed by many others. The pictures of the object resemble the planet Saturn, squashed and elongated. They matter because the Brazilian government's own lab analysis pronounced them genuine, witnesses on land and sea support the reports and also experienced a loss of electrical power as the object sped in front of them. In this case we have a series of consistent photographs showing the progress of a mysterious object with the negatives, the date and time of the pictures and the location itself in absolutely no doubt. The rigour with which the evidence was produced is almost unknown in the UFO world. The captain of the ship hosting Barauna insisted the photographer develop his reel immediately and strip to his swimming trunks to avoid any possibility of his swapping an already exposed roll of film for the one in his camera!

Oregon farmer Paul Trent kept his pants on but over fifty years after he took two photographs of a large object that passed his property on 11 May 1950 the black and white shots have defied the best scientific attempts to discredit them. The generally scathing Condon Committee, a US government-sponsored investigation into UFOs, cited the pictures as the best photographic case in its files. Later computer enhancing suggests the shots show a large object at a great distance. There is no evidence of strings or wires and no tell-tale light pattern indicating a small object at a close distance to the camera. The metallic disc in the pictures does not resemble any aircraft under test at the time that has since gone into service. Indeed, the disc with its off-centre central tower, resembles virtually no aircraft known to man.

Films and videos of alleged UFOs also have their hard core of classic cases. One of the most celebrated is the controversial multiple video sighting surrounding an eclipse seen from Mexico City in July 1991. Many residents of the city recorded the eclipse on their camcorders and a virtual UFO mania took hold when well over a dozen recordings showed a stationary aerial object. At first glance this case was perfect with multiple recordings made from different angles at the same time. The eclipse, clearly evident in the recordings, establishes date and time beyond question. The case soon set the UFO magazines and embryonic Internet coverage alight. There is no doubt that the recordings show something hugely interesting but a sceptical investigation has calmed this seemingly incredible case by suggesting that the videos show two objects. One is almost certainly the planet Venus, visible during the day because of the eclipse. The other is large, distant and apparently stationary. It could be anything, up to and including an alien spacecraft. It does, however, look and behave very much like a weather balloon.[6]

Few filmed objects come from radar-visual cases. One of the most durable cases in the literature took place on 20/21 December 1978 when a television crew from New Zealand filmed airborne lights from on board an Argosy freighter aircraft. The 23,000 frames of 16mm colour film devoted to the Kaikoura lights have never been satisfactorily explained. Much of the media furore at the time was overplayed. For example, one frame in which a light appears to perform an incredible looping manoeuvre is almost certainly down to camera shake. For the most part the film shows the work of a rambling and excited reporter and a cameraman struggling with a vibrating plane, cramped cockpit and equipment demanding his constant attention. What they filmed were distant and small-scale lights in the sky. Poor focus made the lights appear larger than they were to the eye and Channel 10 reporter Quentin Fogarty does add a few cod dramatics to the proceedings with his commentary. The line "Let's hope they're friendly" was the title of his book on the subject. The recording matters because similar lights had, apparently, generated eyewitness sightings and radar reports in the preceding days. Radar reports appeared to match the sightings as they were filmed and later flights with better recording equipment on the same route generated nothing to match the original film.[7]

Some other film, never seen by the public, is known to exist. Gun camera film from RAF aircraft was seen by MOD man Ralph Noyes. He believed that the armed forces knew that UFOs were real. His opinions and the cases that formed his view are coming up later in the book. Also coming up later are the investigations of Project Hessdalen in Norway who filmed airborne lights moving in a remote valley and recorded radar traces of the same objects.

In addition to traces on film and radar, there are several cases in which people and the planet have also been left with a lasting imprint. Landings and direct contact with humans have left burn marks, radiation traces and other damage. Much of this evidence is inconclusive but a handful of cases are spectacular and significant. One of the best concerns the experience of Stefan (Steve) Michalak at Falcon Lake, Manitoba, Canada on 20 May 1967. Michalak, an amateur geologist, approached a landed craft. A door opened and closed on the object as Michalak spoke to the occupants, whom he could hear conversing in some strange language. A hatch opened on the craft and Michalak was blasted by hot gases, sustaining first degree burns. A long and painful scramble to safety finally found him in hospital where a host of medical complications ensued. First degree chest burns formed a grill pattern on Michalak and a range of other symptoms, including imbalances in his blood, suggested some exposure to radiation. Over twenty doctors struggled to find any plausible explanation for health problems that continued for months. No diagnosis or conclusive proof of exposure to radiation was possible and the long-term effects included skin problems and a propensity to blackouts. Other people have also reported health problems as a result of UFO sightings.

UFOs have left traces on the ground. In many cases the late arrival of investigators has limited the credibility of any investigation into such evidence. However, in France there has been co-operation between scientists and the government to establish an investigation bureau. This was set up as GEPAN in 1977 and reconstituted in 1988 as SEPRA, with a more complex role involving monitoring events like the re-entry of spacecraft into French airspace. This organisation has established a formidable reputation for investigative quality. One case in particular is worth considering here. On 8 January 1981 at Trans-en-Provence a landing was reported by a man building a small shed. By the standards of many reports this was a mundane event but the traces on the ground were swiftly examined by a GEPAN team who used laboratory soil analysis, with control checks, to establish small but definite changes in the soil. Amongst the evidence, verified by analytical chemists at two universities, was the unexpected discovery of a high number of negatively charged ions and evidence of carbon polymers in the soil. This event, along with others in the SEPRA files, is well researched, suggesting some phenomena we do not understand, and is available for inspection by other researchers.

GEPAN/SEPRA's work has also demonstrated a high degree of critical thinking and turned up evidence that shames other, less scrupulous, investigators. One vivid ring in a field, believed to be a landing trace of a UFO, was shown to be fungal. Perhaps the most entertaining case in the files involves a crater which appeared overnight in a farmer's field. Meticulous investigation revealed an underground detonation of a 50-year-old Second World War bomb, even tracing its manufacture to England.[8] Burns, markings and residues from alleged landings are plentiful in UFO history. The vast majority of the cases have been investigated by amateur groups and much of the evidence remains inconclusive.

Elsewhere the claims border the very edge of believability. The Massachusetts Institute of Technology hosted a high-profile symposium designed to gain academic kudos for UFO and alien abduction investigation. Journalist CDB Bryan listened in astonishment to claims that aliens had successfully treated AIDS and colour blindness.[9] Conferences regularly hear reports of unexpected pregnancies, confirmed by doctors, which have spontaneously ended. The belief, supported by the claims of leading abduction researchers like Budd Hopkins, John Mack and David Jacobs, is that alien abductors are removing pre-term foetuses to allow them to continue their existence on their craft. Their aim, apparently, is to interbreed with humans and produce a race that may eventually be involved in changing the direction of life on Earth.

Elsewhere, hard physical evidence takes the kind of bizarre twists that will be all too familiar to you by this stage of the proceedings. Like many with an active interest in UFOs I have had my hands in Bob Taylor's trousers! Superb trousers they are. The rugged work trousers of a Scottish forestry foreman. Bob and his trousers became estranged around the time his experience in a forest near Livingstone, Scotland, became a celebrated UFO event. The trousers have become a holy relic of UK UFO investigation.

On 9 November 1979 Taylor encountered a large Saturn-shaped object in a forest clearing. He described this object as fading in and out of view. At times he could see clear through it. Two smaller globes with protrusions, similar to Second World War sea mines, flew towards him at which point a rapid series of events left the forester unconscious and his trousers ripped. Lothian police would later treat the incident as an assault, making it a rarity in UFO case lore. Like Stefan Michalak, Taylor sought medical attention and struggled to make sense of an experience he didn't want. He would later be tricked into a hypnotic regression in which he recounted the whole bizarre experience exactly as he had reported it at the time. Some objective investigation was brought to bear on the evidence. The famous trousers showed outward tears as if ripped mechanically and indentations on the ground corresponded with Taylor's report of the objects seen. No additional tracks into and out of the forest were found to indicate that any conventional forest machinery could have made the indentations at the site of the incident. Tests for other evidence like radiation and residues, however, proved negative.[10]

Taylor's experience is one of many in the case histories of the subject in which odd physical evidence has been combined with an eyewitness report. Some of the best-known are the 'car stop' incidents in which petrol engines (not diesels) are stalled by nearby UFOs. Elsewhere power failures and power surges are reported regularly. In one notable British case from 1978 in Risley, Cheshire, a witness reported a truly bizarre incident involving missing time and damage to a two-way radio in his van. Investigation showed the radio had burned out after an unexplained power surge. Elsewhere, damaged homes, cars and gardens bear repeated witness to the fact that people continually experience something out of the ordinary. Any sceptic suggesting such damage was inflicted by the witnesses in search of publicity is missing the point by several light years. On one occasion I dealt with a man reporting something similar to the missing time incident that led to the burned-out radio reported above. The witness in question was convinced he'd had a genuine and frightening experience. He didn't want to go to the papers. In fact, one of his first requests in dealing with the investigators was that nobody mentioned the event to his wife! This witness, like Bob Taylor and the pancake-gathering Joe Simonton, had encountered something that had shaken his belief in all he knew. His sincerity wasn't in question.

Those were a few of the greatest hits in the search for evidence of alien incursion onto our planet. As I told my colleague as she stubbed out her cigarette outside the college, there is evidence, much more than I've had the space to include here. The tortuous 'evidence for what?' question remains unanswered. We have undoubtedly encountered the inexplicable. The Tunguska case for one almost certainly involves some object entering our atmosphere from space. Elsewhere radar-tracked lights supported by eyewitness and photographic evidence prove that genuine events are occurring beyond the understanding of current science. When the best science has been applied to a handful of these events it has strengthened them. Paul Trent's photographs resemble some classic B-movie depictions of a flying saucer but the best computer analysis suggests that the airborne object shown was large, distant and definitely there when the shutter closed. Some witnesses may lie and manufacture evidence but the first-degree burns of Stefan Michalak and the rips in Bob Taylor's trousers are non-starters in this department.

The definitive answers to the questions posed by the evidence here do not, currently, exist. These cases appear most frequently in the books, videos, magazines and Websites that argue for repeated alien contact with mankind. I'd argue this makes good sense in marketing terms but little sense in terms of objective investigation. In a field of investigation packed with claims lacking any evidence and evidence lacking any credence we have a hard core of cases that withstand investigation. They may eventually lead us to discover atmospheric phenomena we don't understand. They may, as we will soon see, help us to a greater understanding of our own psychology. My own feeling is that these explanations and more are behind the cases quoted in this chapter. Perhaps, when we've explained them all away, we'll be left with one or two crowd pleasers that will have the pro-extraterrestrial crowd screaming "We told you so." If and when that happens my guess is that the sceptics will counter with an argument that starts, "Yeah, but you told us all those other dodgy cases were aliens as well."

3. The UFO Community

So far we've explored a brief history and an overview of the best of the evidence. Now it is time to tackle 'the people problem' I referred to in the introduction.

The meanings we make in UFO investigation often come from the people involved. The evidence may lead us to opinions but in many cases any kind of conclusion remains impossible. Even the best documented cases, like Tunguska, are mysteries. Predictably, we have different opinions arrived at by different people. UFO investigation and the community who remain interested in the subject are most certainly different people. Sometimes that means different as in people with contradictory views and sometimes it means different as in not normal like the rest of us. So it is time to meet the people. Where else can we start but with the one group to whom we owe the most. The people without whom this book, and this subject, would not exist.

The Witnesses

Very little definitive research has been carried out on UFO witnesses. We have some notions about who these people are and how they experience their events. The first points that should be made about the witnesses are that many of the popular notions that surround them are plain wrong. Most of the witnesses I have met are not in it for publicity, money or any kind of vicarious need for attention. They are normal people who have experienced something abnormal. Most never find themselves on the receiving end of an active investigation of their experience. Fewer still report anything to the media.

No totally trustworthy statistic exists by which to measure the numbers of people experiencing UFO events. In the USA the Gallup and Roper Poll organisations have systematically included UFO-related questions within their general polling of the population. In 1985 a figure of 6% of the population indicated they had experienced a UFO event. Almost six years later the figure answering the same question had risen to 14%.[1] By 1990 Gallup had polled the American population with this question four times and Roper twice. Gallup's figures consistently came in higher than Roper's for the same question.

Analysing such raw data verges on the impossible. A UFO event in someone's mind may be an obvious sighting of Venus when explained to an astronomer. Jenny Randles once told me something that many investigators have found to be true. Most sightings exceeding 5 minutes prove to be astronomical events. The best example of such an event may be the videos during the Mexico City eclipse.

One possible explanation for the rise in UFO sightings and the seemingly high percentage of people who have experienced them may be that a rising population means there are more people around to see strange phenomena when they occur. Another possible explanation, roughly supported by other polling information, is that people have been seeing strange things for years but are increasingly predisposed to interpret them as UFO events. A series of polls in the USA indicate that over the last 50 years a greater percentage of the American population has come to hold an opinion on UFOs. The most popular opinions are more widely held than they were half a century ago. Roughly half the American population believes that life exists in outer space and that UFOs are alien craft. Predictably, the real picture is far more complicated and some of these figures rose over 50 years ago, but declined in the last 20 years. We can, however, safely state that the USA have produced the most regular and the most thorough polling on UFO belief in the world. Their population may not be representative of the rest of the planet but they can present us with some insights into the experience of UFO witnesses.

The USA and UK have been home to most of the significant psychological research carried out into UFO witnesses. This research is far from definitive but it does deliver some insights that may form the basis of definitive research in the future. The late Ken Phillips carried out a long-term research project into a range of personal factors of UK witnesses. His reports indicate that many UFO witnesses feel a status inconsistency. Roughly speaking, this means the witnesses experience an awareness that their status in life is out of kilter with their background, experience and/or qualifications. Those who feel satisfaction with their jobs still tend to experience adjustment problems in other areas of their lives.[2] Phillips' investigation, called 'The Anamnesis Protocol' also discovered a high rating for an external locus of control.[3] This indicates that a higher than average percentage of his subjects felt that significant areas of their life were totally out of their control. A crude demonstration of this might involve a tricky work situation in which a management were attempting to implement unpopular working practices. A person inclined towards an external locus of control may resent this as much as any other member of staff but would be more likely to do nothing other than say, "We can't do anything." A large-scale American study of UFO witnesses showed a similar pattern of personality traits to Phillips' UK study.[4]

A more controversial train of thought links UFO experience to the growing psychological literature on Fantasy Prone Personality (FPP), which is a theory suggesting susceptibility to fantasy experiences. The concept of FPPs was first advanced in a research paper in 1981.[5] Since then it has appeared in the more scholarly and less widely read end of the UFO literature. Robert Bartholomew and George Howard's investigation into UFOs and aliens contains a succinct analysis of the link between UFOs and the FPP theory.[6] The idea splits the UFO community along predictable lines. The generally sceptical and serious minds of the academic fringe are genuinely exited by a theory that offers explanations for the perplexing reports of witnesses. The witnesses and those most sympathetic to the idea of aliens, known as the ExtraTerrestrial Hypotheses (ETH), are often fiercely resistant to this intrusive idea from social science. Many witnesses are the most resistant of all, claiming, in effect, that a bunch of academics can't tell them what they experienced. A valid criticism for sure. Some researchers with a track record of using hypnotic regression to uncover abduction stories are also conspicuously opposed to the FPP idea. This much was brought home to me when I appeared alongside Manchester solicitor Harry Harris on a television show. The mention of Fantasy Prone Personality had him pointing out that a doctor had assured him it could not be diagnosed. True, but this misses the point.

The existence of FPP is a theory supported by some evidence. So is the existence of Gulf War syndrome. The theory in both cases has led to accurate predictions and fruitful research but we're still a long way short of proof and, therefore, diagnosis. However, we do appear to be in possession of a useful idea that directly tackles some difficult problems. Superficially at least, FPP fits witness and abduction research very well and leaves doubt about the extraterrestrial origin of some, if not all, abduction reports.

Many abductees have returned with specific information about the origins and purpose of their abductors. This information has been relayed sincerely to researchers, at which point it has often proven to contradict information gathered from other abductions. Predictions gathered in this way are similarly unreliable. Any comprehensive theory of abductions has to account for the bizarre encounters reported by people like Joe Simonton who presented his story every bit as sincerely as modern-day abductees. FPP may begin to explain the general sincerity and the odd way in which the nature of abductions appears to change with popular ideas about UFOs and aliens at any given time. It also provides an explanation that links UFO experiences and the fairy lore of old.

Robert Bartholomew and George Howard spent a chapter of their book, *UFOs And Alien Contact,* comparing the best investigations into FPP with the personality traits outlined in biographies of those experiencing UFO events. The results strongly suggest that UFO experiencers have a greater tendency than the general public towards the traits of the FPP. For example 16% of the general public and 92% per cent of those potentially exhibiting FPP report experiencing psychic phenomena. The figure for those claiming UFO events is 75%. This figure, however, doesn't include the claimed UFO event as a manifestation of psychic phenomena.

To put this in context, nobody is claiming that the bulk of those experiencing UFO events are mad. It is simply that they exhibit traits that in other areas of life, like creative professions, are a positive asset. The best proof for this, oddly, comes from an Internet-published paper attempting to prove that the FPP theory was wrong. The original paper discounted some of the main ideas but the researcher invited an independent evaluator of tests to examine the subjects. The independent evaluator was unaware that the subjects were abductees. In comparison to the general public the subjects were found to have rich mental lives, weak sexual identities, tendencies to paranoia and caution and impaired personal relationships.[7] This is far from a universal appraisal of all abductees but it does suggest that many of those reporting UFO events fall into a group of the population who are short of any full-blown mental illness but do exhibit personality traits that shape their lives.

This much has been evident to some commentators for a while. I once had the chance to communicate with aliens. We don't need to bother with the whole story. The gist of it revolves around a UFO research group who had established a psychic channel to a group of almost 1,000 alien superminds who existed in a form approaching pure spiritual energy within the Earth's atmosphere. Superb stuff, and the most endearing trait of these beings was their willingness to answer questions on anything. I got to ask a few. Some, concerning the existence of God, global warming and other major concerns were given a short shrift. One question concerned the promise of Michael Knighton, chairman of Carlisle United, to get the football team I've followed my entire life into the Premiership within ten years. I doubted the sanity of the chairman's statement then. History has shown that he succeeded in regularly taking us to the fringes of the GM Vauxhall Conference. How, I wondered, would these alien superminds have achieved the Premiership? Their reply still gets laughs in front of a live audience. They suggested baking a cake that contained the wishes of the chairman and feeding it to the players who would then deliver on the pitch. If this truly is wisdom from highly advanced alien superminds then, frankly, I have a problem with it. A workable recipe for any cake that can turn lower league cloggers into the equals of £20 million pound internationals beggars belief. I doubt whether heavyweight boxing or reality game shows could compete in a ratings war with a programme that involved locking half a dozen managers and that cake recipe in one room. I don't, however, doubt the sincerity of the people passing the message back to me. Within the group was a person openly admitting to psychic experiences. A prime admission from those who are prime candidates for FPP. The human channel in question was combining psychic experience and alien contact in the same activity. In the circumstances there are many, me included, who would suggest it is easier to believe in FPP than cakes that turn a carthorse of a centre forward into a soccer God.

None of which proves a thing. At the start of the twenty-first century we have a handful of useful research studies into those experiencing UFO events. The common factors identified suggest that many of these people often share personality traits that make them different and, in some cases, border on the dysfunctional. FPP or no FPP, those reporting UFO events tend to set themselves apart from society. In reality, they may have been out on their own before their UFO experience.

I've regularly referred to the UFO community in this book. You won't find them in a phone book and they don't live in any one place but I'd defend the use of the term for three reasons.

a) One meaning of community is a group of people united by a common interest.

b) I've been using it for years without once being challenged on the grounds that it is inappropriate.

c) The English language doesn't contain a single word complex enough to describe the real situation in the UFO world and 'community' is simply the best alternative.

The community in question contains a range of interests. Scientists undertaking serious research. Interest groups like the military who retain their own particular involvement and mingle with everyone else only when necessary. Active researchers and a great many others who buy the merchandise, turn up at one or two major events and follow the whole business from a distance. All sections of this community, especially the casual members, show a pattern of people coming and going on a regular basis. Given the differences in motivation and involvement of such a diverse group it would be impossible to define a single personality type making up the membership. However, there have been attempts to understand and explain this community.

One notable thing about the research into those inclined to believe in the reality of UFOs and aliens is the way the results correspond to the traits identified in witnesses. Steven Resta's masters dissertation in 1975 examined psychological traits of UFO believers. The researcher found a high score for external locus of control.[8] Martin Kottmeyer built on this notion of the UFO audience feeling that their lives were controlled to suggest that the whole community was an example of an evolving system of paranoid belief.[9] This notion was also central to one major British study. David Morris examined the readers of a literature he labelled 'techno occultism' in his book *The Masks Of Lucifer*.[10] His definition took in works on UFOlogy and other paranormal and spiritual literature. Roughly, the kind of material you'd find in the 'Mind, Body and Spirit' section at Waterstone's. He found a link between an interest in this material and notions of personal status in the readers. His findings suggested that the apocalyptic claims and reinventions of conventional wisdom in works like *Chariots Of The Gods* provided comfort to an audience who were struggling for status in their everyday lives. In the simplest terms, there was a comfort in the UFO realities presented in books because they undermined the hard realities of an everyday world in which this audience were often on the margins. This concept is not new. Morris quoted Vance Packard's seminal research into notions of social class and status. Morris linked his view of techno occultist readers to Packard's concept of a 'limited success class.'[11]

Another classic British study formed a PhD thesis for Shirley McIver at the University of York in 1983. Her examination of those actively involved in the UFO community identified some specific motives and personalities. For example, she looked at the Birdsall brothers, who went on to found and organise Quest International, an organisation that leads the UK market in UFO conferences and merchandise. The brothers' youthful interest in employment as secret agents is one item from McIver's study that their fellow UFOlogists still quote with some amusement. This amusement may be misplaced. If anything, the Birdsall brothers have achieved the essence of their dream with a professional life that includes deliveries of secret material, the chance to break incredible stories to the world and a network of contacts around the world who meet, often in Yorkshire, to discuss what is really going on. Your view of their life depends on the faith you place in Quest International and their generally pro-extraterrestrial message. But those attracted to the life of a secret agent in their early years are often dreaming of being at the cutting edge in an arena of cover-ups, collusion and controlling the world. The Birdsall brothers and their less commercially successful peers are not doing it for Queen and country. They are, however, involved in a crusade for truth and fighting unsympathetic forces who conspire against them. Some of us might question the claims of many in UFO groups about infiltration, tapped telephones, their insider knowledge about UFO wreckage in secret East Anglian hangers and a host of other staple stories. We would, however, be idiots to question their own belief and sincerity.

If one thing unites those in the wider UFO community it is this sincerity. Outside of active group members and buyers of any kind of UFO merchandise we have a fringe of those involved because of other interests. Researchers building careers tend to steer away from UFOlogy because of the academic stigma attached to it. There is no widely available research on the psychological make-up of those involved in UFO research who are not members of groups. Given the professional suicide available from such labours we might usefully suggest that these people stand each side of the line that divides dedication and obsession. It is a crude measure for sure but one lengthy insight into the truth of this suggestion comes from Leo Sprinkle. His autobiographical account of an academic career combined with UFOlogy, *Soul Samples*,[12] details a series of tetchy academic spats and self-justifying soul-searching episodes of his own alongside his groundbreaking work with abductees. Sprinkle was one of the first to pioneer an approach that put UFO experiencers in the centre of investigation and, in effect, allowed them a say in what mattered and how the investigation should proceed. Sprinkle's self-help philosophy allowed him to work with groups of abductees but his motives in doing so bring another dimension to our understanding of those involved in UFO research. Sprinkle is an experiencer himself. In fact, those claiming some kind of experience make up a significant but hard to quantify section of the general UFO community. Leo Sprinkle is one example that shows the blurring of boundaries in this area. He is an experiencer, a delegate and performer at conferences, an avid consumer of merchandise and also a researcher involved in the field in his professional capacity.

Experiences of a different kind form the basis for the involvement of others. Canadian neuroscientist Dr Michael Persinger has developed experiments to prove a theory he advanced in 1977. Persinger believes that electromagnetic energy fields can affect the human brain in a manner that causes UFO experiences. Persinger pursues these investigations in his professional capacity at Laurentian University using custom-built lab equipment. He has produced results that suggest his original theory has much merit. Some other researchers, including Britain's Albert Budden and Paul Devereux, are engaged on very personal quests based on similar beliefs. This is a dedication summed up by Devereux's apology as he ran over time during a presentation to the *Fortean Times Unconvention*, asking the audience to stay with him a few minutes longer he stated simply, "This is the work of a lifetime." Devereux's work on earthlights is based on a belief that natural energies leaked into the atmosphere can form short-lived airborne lights which ride the magnetic fields of the Earth. Budden has developed an 'electro-staging hypothesis' which suggests that Devereux and Persinger are working along the right lines. Budden also studies electromagnetic pollution from sources like mobile phones and radio masts, seeing this as a potential cause of UFO events.

The likes of Devereux and Budden are ambivalent figures in the UFO community because their theories fly in the face of the popular belief in aliens and abductions. Jenny Randles noted in her *Little Giant Encyclopaedia Of UFOs* that Budden had 'left UFOlogy behind to align himself with scientists.' It is a telling comment because Budden has continued to study UFO events but his theories find some derision and limited sales amongst the UFO community. I think he is on to a major truth but I'm struggling to convince others. The obsessive dedication of figures like Albert Budden is in a great scientific pioneer spirit, and the scarcity of serious scientific investigation in UFOlogy has left open the possibility that amateurs can make earth-shattering discoveries. Budden's work overlaps with other studies into electromagnetic pollution that concentrate on the possibility that our expanding communications network is damaging both our mental and physical health.[13]

Military, atmospheric and aeronautical scientists have followed UFO events for many years. More accurately, they have taken a marginal interest but occasionally added theories and ideas to the field which have influenced UFOlogical thinking. The mutual suspicion between the essentially amateur UFO fraternity and those with careers in the military and scientific worlds remains strong. There have been some attempts to bridge the gap. The most accessible is probably Edward Ashpole's book *The UFO Phenomena* (1995).[14] The book, a greatest hits of UFO events with scientific thought added, provides a potted history of some important opinions. Career scientists and military people may exist on the fringes of the UFO community but their work is influential in making meaning and establishing some of the limits of the claims of the UFO researchers. Ashpole notes that of the hundreds of contactee and abduction cases claimed up to 1995, not one had provided 'anything of acceptable scientific interest - say, something on which one could write a paper for *Nature* or *Science*.' Ashpole also puts some current claims into a hard scientific context. For example, quoting Carl Sagan's famous observation when faced with the claims of Antonio Villas Boas to have had sex with an alien. Sagan noted that there was more chance of an elephant mating with a petunia than a human mating with an extraterrestrial. Ashpole notes the biological improbability of our species venturing easily into an alien atmosphere. 'Sadly the scenarios of *Star Trek* are wrong. Spock reports to Captain Kirk that the planet's atmosphere is breathable... in reality, one whiff of that 'breathable' atmosphere could end a promising career in Star Fleet Command. And maintaining control of our bowels on Planet-X could be an embarrassing problem never faced by Captain Kirk and his crew.'

Scientific and military views are advanced to some derision amongst the UFO community. The Search for ExtraTerrestrial Intelligence (SETI) is a project with its own institute in California. A methodical search for evidence of extraterrestrial communications based on radio astronomy, the Institute exists uneasily alongside popular views in the UFO community. If the claims of just one abductee are proven then the SETI Institute is nothing short of a multimillion dollar international embarrassment. SETI scientists, by contrast, are generally sympathetic to the wishes of the popular UFO writers and researchers but unimpressed with the quality of their evidence or argument.

There is much animosity between military investigation and the UFO community. Officially many world governments, including those of the USA and UK, admit to investigating UFOs but state that their interest ends when they have examined the defence implications of any specific case. Popular opinion in the UFO community sees this as spin-doctoring at best and, quite probably, an outright lie. Others, including the late Ralph Noyes, who spent his career in the Ministry of Defence, claim otherwise. Noyes was active in the UFO community for years and consistent in his stated view that the Ministry had UFO evidence which had not been made available to the public. Noyes believed that the MOD had conclusive proof that UFOs were real and that they were not alien spacecraft. Their real nature, he said, remained elusive. But it was, apparently, clear to MOD investigators that some of the most incredible UFO events were being caused by unknown atmospheric phenomena. In such a situation the covert infiltration of some UFO groups by the military and their own interest in spiriting the best cases away from the public would make some sense. Noyes was adamant that only three cases had ever really got the military nervous during his tenure, two of these will be dealt with in detail later.

Considering the UFO community in the light of Noyes' comments it is possible to see how suspicion and hostility might build between military and amateur researchers. Rank and file researchers would be right to believe in infiltration and secrecy. For their part the military would feel justified. As we will see later, the cases that made the military nervous concerned UFOs behaving in a manner that caused initial fears about an incoming military strike. The possibility that the nation could be panicked into launching a military strike against an unknown atmospheric phenomena raises public relations issues. More alarmingly, there is the possibility that an outbound missile strike could be on its way before we knew for sure that it was only UFOs coming the other way.

Making Meaning About UFOs

We've spent little time considering the cases in this chapter but what we have here is important. It matters because we need to remind ourselves of some vital points relating to the evidence. Firstly, UFOs and UFO information are very much a commercial enterprise. Most of the information in the public domain is there because it makes commercial sense. The best-selling information, like the puzzling cases and the idea of aliens being present on this planet, gets regular exposure and frequent media makeovers. The dedicated research in academic disciplines like psychology is discussed in a few peer-reviewed journals and given bookshop space only in the largest and most eclectic stores. The unchecked Internet is alive with UFO information, most of it in the conspiracy/"they're here" category.

The illusion of UFO publications, Websites and videos is that they present hard information all the time. In reality, we are often dealing with infotainment, a situation in which the facts are shaped to market needs. The truth can be a casualty. People make their own meanings by deciding on the information they receive. Groups may then gather and support each other's beliefs. Not surprisingly, the most popular beliefs remain popular and the cult areas stay on the fringes. This is a situation closer to popular entertainment than an information-based pursuit. In entertainment some staple products, like soap operas, remain popular and repeat aspects of their winning formulae. In information-based pursuits, like an educational course, there is a more linear structure and the goal is a conclusion or achievement. Those with a UFO interest often talk like an educational course and behave like a soap opera.

Ironically, one person to recognise this situation is Timothy Good, the best-selling author who made a fortune from pro-extraterrestrial and pro-conspiracy writing. Promoting the massive-selling *Beyond Top Secret* in 1996, Good told *The Guardian*, "If ever there's a subject that needs rescuing from its supporters, it's this one."

Good's comment and the work of pollsters and psychologists would suggest that there may be such a thing as a UFO-related state of mind. More accurately, there may be a popular mythology at work in people's minds. Those inclined to believe their lives are controlled from outside may be the most susceptible. They may also be well represented in the regular audience for UFO material that feeds this very belief. Admittedly, there is little psychological research but the most comprehensive work is quoted here and does show a consistency of results between studies and between the groups of UFO experiences and the audience for material on UFOs. The most significant thing about this work is the consistency in the key areas of external locus of control. It also shows a general belief in UFOs and extraterrestrial life. Two highly-controversial experiments have added some insight into how these facts might manifest themselves.

At the Anaheim Memorial Hospital, California, in 1977 Alvin Lawson and William McCall conducted a survey using hypnosis. They took 16 subjects, some genuine abductees and some who had been previously screened and selected for their lack of interest in UFOs. Through a series of questions they made the subjects imagine and recount tales of encounters with UFOs. The experiment found many and distinct similarities between the stories told by the abductees and those with little interest. Both groups were encouraged to see the events as real. In 1993 the British researcher John Spencer attempted something similar and found similar results.[15]

These small-scale studies remain controversial, not least because of the ethical position of leading those with little or no belief in UFOs to believe they have had genuine experiences. However, the experiments do open the possibility that the public at large have a mental template of a UFO experience. This, in theory, could be triggered by an event or some effect on their brain, as suggested by researchers like Persinger, Devereux and Budden. These experiments and the other material on the make-up of those experiencing UFO contacts also suggest that much UFO-related experience may be psychological. This may present a model in which the personalities and their experiences remain the same over a long period and their interpretations vary with the ideas of a particular society. In short, this is a view that links fairy experiences of the past with present-day UFO events and begins to explain why countries like the USA and UK seem to experience a certain kind of abduction whilst other cultures, like black Africa, report very different experiences and far fewer UFOs.

This view puts UFOs and alien abductions into realm of study that includes paranoid ideas and panics of all kinds. For example, Asia's koro epidemics, in which men become convinced that they are afflicted by a contagious disease causing their penises to shrink. Koro resembles UFO events in that reports come from frighteningly sincere individuals and find themselves supported by occasional widespread outbreaks of general belief and mass reporting. The concentration on Asia would suggest a social dimension but there are cases around the world. In the Pocket Essential on *Conspiracy Theories* Robin Ramsay reported an encounter with a scary individual who believed himself to be a robot whose every action was controlled from outside. He also believed that some unspecified people had broken into his house and substituted his penis for a smaller one![16]

There is nothing approaching a definitive investigation into how and why people see UFOs, but the tight consistency in a few studies is good evidence for there being a strong psychological component behind some experiences. However, as with all strands of UFOlogical thought, there are obvious limits. These UFO state of mind theories look useful against some reports and facts. They are of limited use in explaining what put the burns on Stefan Michalak's chest. They don't begin to explain what exploded over Tunguska in 1908. Most importantly, you might reject these explanations if you woke up tomorrow morning with a strange memory of some bedroom visitor.

So, bear this research in mind because it is useful and it is all we have to help us understand how and why these things may happen to people.

4. Amazing Tales

The debates and the different angles have been considered, and we know it is unlikely that there will be any kind of agreement across the UFO community because this business often means what each community member decides what it means. It's time to examine a few cases. This chapter has some of UFOlogy's greatest hits and the next examines some strange and perplexing events. Armed with the insights gained so far, the conclusions are yours for the making.

Roswell

If UFOlogy has its own *Citizen Kane* or *Pet Sounds*, an event so epoch making that everyone is obliged to have an opinion, that case is Roswell. Little is certain here. All we can safely say is that some event occurred in the summer of 1947 and by early July its significance was obvious to the highest-ranking elements of the US Army Air Force (USAAF) stationed at Roswell. Deemed insignificant for years, even by UFO investigators, the case took on monumental importance after its rediscovery in the late 1970s. Now the claims surrounding the event are pivotal to the standing of UFO investigation.

It is claimed that on or around 1 July 1947 unknown targets appeared on the radar screens at White Sands Proving Grounds, a top secret Army Air Force facility near Roswell, New Mexico. In the following days at least one local couple saw a glowing object pass overhead and rancher WW 'Mac' Brazel heard a loud explosion during a violent thunderstorm. Later, he discovered a debris field made up of lightweight materials including printed shreds covered, apparently, in floral designs, 'I' shaped beams of balsa-like wood, tough metal foil and some 'hieroglyphics.' He took the material to neighbours Floyd and Loretta Proctor who suggested he turn it in to Sheriff George Wilcox. The Sheriff notified Roswell Army Air Force (RAAF) Colonel William Blanchard who, in turn, despatched intelligence officer Major Jesse Marcel to interview the rancher and inspect the debris. Brazel, Marcel and counter-intelligence operative Captain Sheriden Cavitt headed out to the debris field, spending a day collecting material. At the Roswell base Colonel Blanchard decided to have the wreckage shipped to Wright Field in Ohio. He also oversaw a press announcement to the local media which stated that RAAF had in their possession a "flying disc." Predictably, this caused an instant sensation. As the debris stopped over at Fort Worth on their way to Ohio, General Roger Ramey took charge of affairs, ordering a press release stating that the material was nothing more significant than a crashed weather balloon. Wreckage consistent with this claim was displayed by Major Marcel in front of the press.

At this point the case went quiet for over 30 years after which, claims and counter-claims would cloud the real facts. Today some claim that Roswell was the site of the crash of an alien spacecraft, with some stories suggesting that at least one live alien was recovered. Other stories claim a number of dead aliens were retrieved, although the number varies with the person telling the story. Circumstantial evidence and a series of supporting witnesses support these pro-extraterrestrial claims. An alternative argument points to inconsistencies in the witness testimony and the conspicuous failure of the hard evidence produced to date to support this fantastic story. This generally sceptical camp see Roswell as a secret military operation that misfired, basing their argument on several key facts. It is an uncanny coincidence that aliens just happened to crash near the only fully operational nuclear bomber base on Earth, and were almost within sight of a key testing area for top secret military equipment. The one strand of evidence that is used in both the pro-UFO and sceptical cases is a series of changes in the official explanations. These indicate that military authorities have been inclined to cover-up and mislead. Beyond that, what these changes in the official line prove is up for debate.

One of the most ironic facts pertaining to this case is that the most vivid and widely disseminated versions of the story now disagree with the facts that started the whole craze. The widely accepted stories place the date of the UFO crash in early July but the one interview on record with Mac Brazel makes it clear that he found the debris in mid-June, he simply took it to the local Sheriff on his next visit to town, around the Independence Day weekend. Similarly, there is doubt over the testimony of almost every key witness. Jesse Marcel, whose interview with UFOlogist Stanton Friedman led to the revival of the story, overstated his qualifications and experience whilst giving interviews to UFO investigators. He was widely ridiculed in the USAAF at the time of the Roswell incident for his own belief that the event was a flying saucer crash.

One other witness, local mortician Glenn Dennis, told a story that appeared convincing because it didn't present him as central or heroic. He claimed he had received phone calls seeking information about preserving bodies exposed to the elements for some time and requesting small sealed caskets. Subsequently, he had to drive an injured airman to the Roswell base. After delivering his human cargo he went in search of a girlfriend who worked as a nurse on the base. At the base hospital he realised things were out of the ordinary because of the presence of military police. His girlfriend emerged, clearly distressed and seemed horrified to see Dennis, warning him to get away because he could "get killed" for sticking around. The pair, Glenn Dennis claimed, met for a drink the following week at which point the nurse told him she had been assisting at the autopsy of a dead alien. Dennis named the nurse as Naomi Selff, claiming she had been killed in an air crash following a British posting. Her whereabouts and real identity became a brief fixation in UFOlogy. Initially, writers like Donald Schmitt claimed that the records of nurses at the Roswell base were unobtainable. By 1995 journalist Pete McCarthy had located the records, easily as it transpired, and tracked down the one surviving nurse, Rosemary McManus. McCarthy was able to prove that McManus knew nothing of any retrieval of alien bodies and had never heard of Dennis' girlfriend Naomi Selff. Glenn Dennis is also a founder and stakeholder in the Roswell International UFO Museum And Research Centre.

Apart from Jesse Marcel there are a handful of others who claim direct involvement in retrieving debris or discovering the crash. All claim some variation on a story that suggests more than one crash site with a smattering of debris falling onto the ranch where Mac Brazel discovered it. In these accounts there were one or two other crash sites on which an entire craft, or virtually entire craft, hit the ground. The odd thing about these witnesses, Gerald Anderson, Jim Ragsdale, Frank J Kaufman and Grady L 'Barney' Barnett is that none reported seeing the other witnesses at the site. Their testimony also differs in significant aspects of the case. Barnett's story was told by his friends Mr and Mrs Vernon Malthais because Barnett himself was dead. The disagreement in the stories has been taken by some to prove the worthlessness of the case. This is a little simplistic. Beyond doubt some of these witnesses are lying. All, however, introduced key elements to the story that have found at least one supporter.

Barney Barnett's account was the first to mention the presence of an archaeological team, working in the area, who had happened upon the crash site. Gerald Anderson was instrumental in supporting the surviving alien claim. Frank J Kaufman's story is incredible, placing him at the centre of events from the initial radar tracking, through the recovery of the craft, to the highly classified cover-up operation. Some of the more charitable researchers into the case claim that the length of time that has passed is bound to confuse memories. Maybe. But the fact remains that, to date, the Roswell case is saddled with an incredible story at its heart, key witnesses who disagree, a flexible number of crash sites and absolute confusion over the definitive date of the event. One key witness, Jim Ragsdale, moved the crash site in his testimony after a local UFO museum was refused permission to buy the original location as he described it. It is easy to be cynical but Ragsdale made his revised statement when he knew he was terminally ill. His video and book *The Jim Ragsdale Story*, in which the crash site was a crucial aspect, were intended to benefit his grandchildren.

We may dismiss much of the witness testimony but Roswell remains a live case because some witnesses are harder to put down and the official explanations are contradictory. Two military witnesses should be considered. Oliver 'Pappy' Henderson was a noted practical joker and his alleged UFO fragment shown to a fishing buddy was, in all probability, from a crashed V2 rocket. Pappy, however, confided in his wife that he had flown top secret wreckage to Wright Field in 1947. It is beyond doubt that such a flight did take place and went unreported at the press conference presenting the weather balloon explanation. Henderson was one of the USAAF's top pilots with a history of involvement in essential missions. He would have been a likely candidate for such an operation.

In 1990 Brigadier General Arthur E Exon approached researchers Kevin Randle and Donald Schmitt with the story they wanted to hear. Highly decorated, with a service history commanding Wright Field, which was renamed Wright Patterson Air Force Base in the 1960s. Exon, apparently, confirmed everything. Varied crash sites, recovery of bodies, confirmation of incredible properties of the recovered material and the clincher, the resulting investigation had established alien origin. Exon's standing appeared to put the matter beyond doubt. Randle and Schmitt's books *UFO Crash At Roswell* (1991) and *The Truth About The UFO Crash At Roswell* (1994) are consistent with Exon's story. But some key points should be noted. Exon made it clear that he had heard his stories as rumours and his timings are a little vague in the areas of key events, making it possible that he heard the rumours years after the alleged events. Exon himself wrote to Randle and Schmitt complaining they represented his account as fact when he had made clear its origin as rumour. Exon is disregarded by some commentators who don't trust his story. Others think his testimony may be intended to provide a case study in the credulous nature of UFO reporting. If so, the fact that those who quote him often treat his story as fact rather than rumour, has probably proven the point.

Exon's story is probably less fantastic than some of the official explanations to have emerged over the years. The United States Air Force (USAF) published *The Roswell Report: Fact Vs Fiction In The New Mexico Desert* in 1993, the same year that an investigation by the General Accounting Office (GAO) was started. The GAO is, in effect, America's Ombudsman's Department. The USAF settled on a combination of a misidentified Project MOGUL balloon and subsequent hysteria as their explanation. Project MOGUL was a top secret undertaking in which weather balloons were used to carry sensors, overfly the USSR and detect atomic explosions. The 1995 GAO report established that most information management had been handled correctly. The report was in response to a Freedom Of Information Act request filed by UFO researcher Karl Pflock. The GAO were not charged with discovering the truth of the event. They did discover that the pattern of communications traffic centred on the event showed no indication of a truly significant occurrence sufficient to demand attention at the highest level. UFO investigators seized on the discovery that the administrative records for the Roswell base between 1945 and 1949 appeared to have been destroyed. In 1997 the USAF followed their first investigation with a wider study, *The Roswell Report: Case Closed*. In a typical UFO community twist the *Case Closed* report gave new life and heart to the very investigators it sought to silence. The new report attempted to explain reports of military cordons and bodies in the witness testimony, concluding that mishaps in experiments with human dummies strapped to high altitude balloons had been the basis for these reports. The experiments and mishaps did occur but not until years after the alleged Roswell crash. The US Air Force said mistakes in witness memory in the intervening period had linked the dummy crashes with Roswell stories.

Whatever the intention, the second Air Force report was a welcome development for the pro-extraterrestrial contingent whose case was in danger of being buried by contradictions by 1997. The loopholes in the official explanation convinced many that a desperate cover-up was still in place. Another view of this was succinctly stated by Lynn Picknett: "The question is whether the USAF investigation set out to explain things that didn't need to be explained in the first place."

Picknett's position is probably the most pragmatic in the circumstances. She supports the MOGUL balloon theory which does stand up well against the proven facts. In this scenario Mac Brazel discovered unusual weather balloon debris in mid-June as a result of the failure of a top secret experiment. The MOGUL project was central to US monitoring of Russia. When it became obvious to the USAAF that one of their top secret rigs had crashed to earth the rash decision was taken to mislead the public with the "flying disc" press release. In any case, one of their own men, Marcel, had mistakenly jumped to this conclusion. The furore caused by the press release demanded some hasty backtracking and whilst the 'weather balloon' press conference was being held with genuine balloon fragments gathered by Brazel, preparations were under way to fly the top secret apparatus suspended beneath the balloons to Wright Field. In this scenario almost all of the rest of the alleged evidence is a tissue of lies hell-bent on securing fame and money. In which case one of Roswell's sternest critics, John Keel, is right in stating that the case is "A boil on the ass of UFOlogy."

The only other workable explanation is that the case continues to be classified at the highest level because somewhere in the morass of disagreement and disharmony there is a truth so monumental that, to date, the few who genuinely know have deemed it too explosive to share with the rest of the world.

Roswell has spawned a series of books and anyone with a spare month on their hands is recommended to take them in along with the copious Internet coverage and *Roswell: The UFO Cover Up*, a 1994 TV movie starring Kyle McLachlan (aka Special Agent Dale Cooper in *Twin Peaks*) as Major Marcel. Martin Sheen and country music legend Dwight Yoakam also turn in impressive performances. If you are still hungry for more there are the alleged landing site(s) and Roswell's three UFO museums.[1]

Murmurs In The Ministry

According to former MOD man Ralph Noyes the following cases were amongst the handful that had his employers in a genuine state of anxiety. 20 years apart, neither case has ever been satisfactorily solved. On the odd occasion that I'm asked for a favourite and/or best UFO case ever I'll quote one of these.

At 9.30 p.m. on 13 August 1956 radar operators at RAF Bentwaters picked up a target over the North Sea moving towards the base at incredible speed. Estimates would later place the velocity around 4950 mph. Nothing man-made could move that fast in 1956. When this object vanished from the scope 18 other targets, led by a group of three, appeared. Once again moving inland from the sea, the second wave were on a different trajectory and moving more slowly. A T-33 aircraft, vectored to investigate, saw nothing. The cluster of targets then appeared to group together to form one target, giving a stronger radar echo than any known aircraft. The radar returns were unbelievable but their consistency had long since convinced the radar staff they were dealing with something real.

The large object was followed on radar until it vanished. Soon afterwards a target moving at the same incredible speed as the first was detected. Just before 11 o'clock the staff in the radar tower saw the object out of the windows. The presence of something strange in the sky was also confirmed by the pilot of a C-47 transport aircraft who reported a bright light streaking underneath his aircraft. Within minutes an open line had been established between radar operation rooms covering Norfolk and Suffolk at Bentwaters, Lakenheath and Sculthorpe. Lakenheath located and tracked a target that alternated stationary periods with movement between 400 and 600 mph. Training Sergeant Forrest D Perkins at Lakenheath Air Traffic Control was co-ordinating the radio traffic and was able to establish that a separate radar operation monitoring ground approach in the same area also had the object on their scopes. This tracking alone struck him as bizarre given the presence of a Moving Target Indicator (MTI) on the radar equipment. This should have disregarded stationary objects. One possible explanation for the continued tracking of a stationary object is that the whole object was rotating or showing rapid movement on its surface.

An air intercept was ordered and a Venom aircraft from RAF Water-beach near Cambridge was scrambled. By midnight the pilot had visual contact and his radar operator had a lock on the object. The pilot reported, "I've got my guns on him." Within seconds the pilot had lost sight and his radar operator was reporting that the object had moved rapidly behind them. Confused and, quite possibly, frightened the pilot called for instructions but the operators manning the military scopes had never seen anything like the movement of the object. Trained to monitor combat, they recognised the development as potentially hostile but couldn't advise on a strategy for the pilot. The obvious response, scrambling a second Venom, was effected. Within a short time the object had vanished from all but one of the scopes. This development is also significant. The object hadn't vanished. In all probability it had just been seen by civilians on the ground with the Venom in pursuit. Only Laken-heath's Air Traffic Control radar had the capability of monitoring low level manoeuvres. They followed the object for a further five minutes as it pursued the first Venom and then stopped at very low altitude once again, before disappearing from the scope for good. The second Venom, arriving on the scene later, got no visual or radar lock.[2]

Just over 20 years later a similar event shook the UK and US military, and the Iranian Air Force who experienced it first-hand. At 12.30 a.m. on 19 September 1976 the occupants of the Shemiran area of Tehran reported a brilliant light overhead. Initially sceptical of the reports, Deputy Commander Of Operations BG Yousefi received a report from the local Mehrabad Air Traffic Control that they had a track of the object. Yousefi went outside and saw the object for himself. By 1.30 he had ordered an F-4 Phantom from Shahrokhi Air Force Base to intercept. 25 miles from the object the pilot had visual and radar confirmation of his target. Having confirmed a radar lock he was stunned to see all his instrumentation, along with the UHF and VHF radio, fail at the same moment. Helpless to do anything other than fly the plane he headed for base. All his suspect systems returned to full working order halfway back to the runway.

Another F-4 was already on its way. The second aircraft, piloted by Lieutenant Jafari, got a lock around 27 miles. Jafari and the UFO were both travelling at speed but his instruments indicated he was gaining on the object at 150 mph. The fighter was travelling well above this speed, indicating the object was moving quickly away from the aircraft. The radar return on his scope indicated the object to be around the same size as a Boeing 707 tanker aircraft. Soon the object shot away. Jafari, breaking the sound barrier on full afterburner, tried to close the distance. Then things took a turn for the worse.

A small object detached itself from the large target and flew directly towards the F-4. Jafari armed an air-to-air AIM 9 (Sidewinder) missile to respond to this apparent rocket attack. Within seconds his plane, like the other F-4, was in the throes of a full systems failure with the unwelcome complication of an imminent impact. Jafari took desperate evasive action, hurling the fighter into a rapid turn and dive manoeuvre. The small object followed the Phantom at a distance of 3-4 miles before returning towards the larger UFO. Whatever this small object had been it certainly wasn't the simple air-to-air missile Jafari feared. The Phantom's systems returned but Jafari wasn't about to attempt another attack.

The large UFO released a second object which headed down into the desert. Jafari and his navigator watched, expecting a missile explosion. They saw a new object appear to soft-land on the ground before bathing a few square miles of desert with bright light. Homing in on the location of the landing, Jafari noticed pulsing electrical interference, possibly from the object. Fifty miles away an airliner coming into Tehran reported a similar problem identifying the source along the same compass bearing as reported by Jafari.

Whatever the cause, the brilliant glow of the object had damaged Jafari's night vision to the point that Shahrokhi had to guide him back in. He needed several circuits over the base before he was ready to land. The following day the crew of the second F-4 were helicoptered to the desert location. The occupants of the only house for miles reported hearing a loud noise and seeing a brilliant light the previous night.[3]

In an utterly incredible twist to this case researchers Jenny Randles and Peter Hough talked to Dr Simon Taylor, a British university lecturer, then engaged and now married to an Iranian woman. Camping out on a mountain top near Tehran just hours before the mid-air incident he had experienced an event almost beyond description. Phrases like 'altered state of consciousness' barely do justice to an incident in which the lecturer and a friend found themselves open to surreal experiences that bordered on dreams, leaving them with short-term problems of adjustment and some longer-term health problems.[4]

To date, no widely accepted explanation is available for the Bentwaters or Tehran cases. Other similar tales exist but these two are, arguably, the best given the range of evidence from radar to eyewitness, the length of the sightings, the number of witnesses and the proven presence in both events of supporting documentation from military sources. Ralph Noyes was adamant that the MOD knew more about UFOs than they were prepared to admit. He was also convinced they had established that UFOs were not extraterrestrial and were atmospheric phenomena.

Whatever the cause, these cases hint at a phenomena which appears to display intelligence and a direct ability to respond to unwanted human investigations. Regardless of the cause, these were events that caused concern in military circles, not least because in their initial stages, they resembled hostile military activity.

Bass, How Low Can You Go?

Another worrying case occurred on 21 October 1978. 20-year-old Frederick Valentich, an amateur pilot who dreamed of flying professionally, had hired a Cessna 182 for a short return flight from Moorabin Airfield near Melbourne to King Island. He intended to pick up crayfish. He filed a flight plan but an unexplained trip from the airfield rendered this useless and ensured he would arrive at King Island after dark. Once airborne the young pilot began to ask Air Traffic Control (ATC) about unknown aircraft in his area. Flying below 5,000 feet he was off the radar scope. So was the bright green light he described flying over and above him. The radio recording of Valentich's conversations with Steve Robey at ATC is one of UFOlogy's most puzzling artefacts. As the event escalates and Valentich reports his engine rough idling other comments are made. "It's not an aircraft, it's..." Valentich never completed that sentence. Valentich had remained calm but his final communications to ATC showed obvious fear in his voice. "That strange aircraft is hovering on top of me again... It is hovering and it is not an aircraft... Delta Sierra Juliet, Melbourne..." A burst of noise, variously identified as carrier wave interference and 'metallic scraping' closed the communication for good.

To date no trace of Valentich or the Cessna have been found. In May 1982 the official Australian investigation concluded, 'The reason for the disappearance... has not been determined.' There has been a lot of speculation in the UFO community. Sceptics point out that Valentich had an active interest in UFOs, his disappearance from the airfield ahead of the flight was never explained and he took much more fuel than he needed. In addition, he was an inexperienced pilot attempting a difficult night landing and had failed to carry out a standard procedure, calling ahead to King Island to ensure the runway was illuminated. In short, these facts might suggest he was planning a major UFO hoax. Those closest to the pilot find this incredible and the facts of his generally happy life don't support any such drastic move. In any case, he still had time to radio ahead and he spent much of his short flight being bemused and then frightened by the strange light. Some theories don't stand up. One explanation suggests the young pilot became confused and ended up flying upside down and looking at his own lights in the Bass Strait. Possible, but highly unlikely when you consider that his light plane survived for over six minutes in such circumstances.

One intriguing theory, advanced by Dr Richard Haines, suggests that Valentich might have fallen foul of a covert military experiment which generated the light phenomena. There is some circumstantial evidence for this in a series of events in places like Orford Ness on the East Anglian coast where light phenomena, experiments in Star Wars technology, and some unexplained air accidents have occurred in close proximity.

Nothing, or course, has been proven. The Bass Strait is very deep and, whatever the cause, the likelihood is that Valentich and his plane went into those waters just after his last radio communication. The depth and inaccessibility of the wreck have probably kept it from the search teams. Whether the discovery of the wreckage would bring us any closer to an understanding of this chilling case is debatable.[5]

Aldershot Albert Abducted

As we have seen, the debate on abductions is fierce. Admit hypnotic regression into the argument and you have some researchers claiming millions of abductees worldwide. Other researchers, along with professionals in areas like psychotherapy, now accept the dangers of hypnosis. Successful prosecutions have already resulted against those who have treated people on the basis of hypnotically-retrieved memories.

Forget every case that involved hypnosis and forget those in which the witness may conceivably have been led by a researcher with his or her agenda and you eliminate many abductions. Now rule out any remaining abductee who gained notable status, fame or money through their experience. This reduces us to a basic hard core of cases. But they do exist. As I mentioned earlier, I met one experiencer whose fear of notoriety led him to demand that his wife never found out. I couldn't prove his event as an abduction. But the following case does count as an abduction, and it still stands if we rule out everything listed in this paragraph.

In the early hours of the morning on 12 August 1983, 77-year-old Alfred Burtoo was fishing beside the Basingstoke Canal in Aldershot. He saw a light approaching in the sky and noticed that it dropped out of sight some distance from him. Soon two beings, humanoid in appearance, around four feet tall and dressed in coveralls, appeared and beckoned him to follow them. They went to a landed object that Burtoo would later sketch. Broadly similar to the typical saucer designs, the object did have odd ski type legs. Burtoo described the object as black inside and like burnished aluminium on the outside. A voice, from a source he couldn't see, spoke to him. "What is your age?" it asked. Burtoo pointed out he would be 78 on his next birthday. "You are too old and infirm for our purpose," replied the voice. Soon afterwards Burtoo departed, walked back to his seat on the canal bank and was happily chasing fish when the object departed with a bright glow. The glow was so bright it allowed Burtoo to see his float bobbing near the far bank of the canal. Burtoo had lived a tough and eventful life. He'd seen military service including active duties in World War Two. He'd also trapped and hunted in Canada, tackling bears and wolves. He suffered no obvious physical effects from his UFO encounter but did admit that turning the events over in his mind caused him problems getting to sleep. He died aged 80 having consistently told the same story to family, friends and the odd UFO researcher.

If Alfred Burtoo was lying he went against the habits of a lifetime, misled a wife with whom he'd enjoyed a long and happy marriage and deceived the many people who respected him as a local historian. In return his greatest achievement was fleeting fame in a local Aldershot paper. He made it into a million-selling book, but not until he was already dead. If he was telling the truth then he presents us with an apparent paradox. We have a craft and beings who possess a technology well ahead of our own and the ability to concoct a mission that seems both complex and important. They jeopardise the lot because their advanced abilities still leave them unable to tell a pensioner with a fishing line apart from younger and fitter specimens of humanity.[67]

The cases in this chapter hint at incredible truths. Roswell may remain debatable but the other events are less so. The events in this chapter are not unique, but they are rare. Such events remain the basis for the most incredible beliefs and claims in UFOlogy. In the next chapter we will examine some lesser-known events which may also teach us important lessons about UFOs and why we see them.

5. Cautionary Tales

UFOlogy is partly infotainment - information gathered into market-friendly packages. The best-selling books on UFOlogy deal with abductions and the belief that UFOs are alien spacecraft. This is possible but not proven, even by cases like the Tehran incident. As we have seen already in this book, the answers may come from some unlikely areas. Here are some examples.

"The Wings And Engine Of A Flying Saucer."

On 21 March 1953 a top-secret shipment arrived in New York aboard the USS General Greely. Two days later the cargo was safely deposited in Fort Knox, Kentucky, where it would remain for a quarter of a century. Prior to the sailing of the USS General Greely from Bremerhaven in Germany, the cargo had been under top secret American guard in Austria. The men guarding the cargo as it moved were told they were transporting "The wings and engine of a flying saucer." This much is undisputed fact because it is confirmed by a declassified memo from the US State Department. The memo has been declassified because there is no longer any need for secrecy in this case.

The boxes contained the crown jewels of Hungary, including the Crown of St Stephen. This one relic alone is now officially priceless. When it did have an estimable value the price was an astronomical $300 million, and that was in the 1930s. Spirited away from Hungary by patriots who didn't want the relics to fall into Communist hands, the treasures were eventually returned by US President Jimmy Carter in 1978. Today they are on public view in Budapest.

So half a century ago the American State Department lied to its own servicemen, albeit for reasons of security. These lies were UFO stories and today the stories resemble several widely believed UFO tales. Some crash retrieval stories have identified Fort Knox as the location of extraterrestrial wreckage. But the highly fortified bullion depository is an impractical place to carry out any kind of investigation on such material. Other elements of the story - the top secret movement of sealed cargo, the minimal briefings given to those guarding the material and the need for a highly secure destination - are a mainstay of the best-known crash retrieval stories.

We know this story is true because the return of the treasures to a politically secure homeland has released classified documentation. We don't know how influential the State Department's cover story became in the development of the crash retrieval legends that fill books and Websites today. There are other stories and other servicemen swearing they moved alien artefacts to top secret locations. Some of these people may be after publicity but others are certainly telling the truth as they know it. Or, more accurately perhaps, the truth as they were told it.[1]

"Can't You See Him?"

On or around 22 February 1973 one of the strangest and potentially most significant abduction events in UFO history occurred. Whilst the exact date of this event has been lost in claim and counter-claim there is no doubt about the start of the abductee's involvement in UFO experiences. Maureen Puddy's first UFO encounter occurred on 3 July 1972 around 9:15 p.m. as she drove to visit her son in hospital just south of Melbourne, Australia. Seeing the road bathed in blue light she initially thought the source was a helicopter, similar to the one in which her son had been carried. When the light appeared to be following her she stopped, got out and saw a large craft which caused her to panic. An 8-mile chase ensued which Maureen Puddy reported to the police and the Royal Australian Air Force. She later had other experiences including further sightings and telepathic contact with a being aboard a UFO. In late February 1973 she had arranged to meet UFO investigators Judith Magee and Paul Norman at a remote spot where, previously, she had experienced her car stopping during a strange encounter. On the way to the meeting Puddy saw a spaceman in a golden suit appear and disappear from her car.

Puddy was reporting this experience to Magee and Norman at their designated meeting spot when her spaceman appeared again. "There he is. Can't you see him?" said Puddy, but the two investigators saw nothing. Things got stranger. The two investigators were sat in the back of Puddy's car as she described her visitor moving outside. Norman got out of the car and walked round. Puddy claimed the spaceman had moved to allow Norman to pass. Then, with the two UFO researchers in the back seat of her car, Puddy appeared to experience a full-blown abduction. Starting apparently conscious, she later went into a faint but still managed to relay details of an event that we would recognise today as a fairly normal abduction. She claimed to be aboard the spaceman's craft but she remained firmly visible in the driving seat as far as Magee and Norman were concerned.

Maureen Puddy went through a range of emotions, ending up in tears at one point as she was told by her hosts aboard the UFO that she would remember nothing of the incident. The two researchers remembered and recorded everything, although the exact date has since confused them! Puddy had other experiences, receiving mainly ridicule as a result. Like many abductees she felt confused and bewildered by the way the phenomena appeared to have chosen her. Her experiences pre-date the era when UFO abductions were a widely known event. In Australia in the early 1970s public knowledge of UFO events was sketchy.

What exactly happened to a woman who described herself as a 'housewife' remains a mystery. Researchers like Albert Budden claim Puddy as someone suffering hypersensitive reactions to electromagnetic events. In this scenario we are dealing with hallucinations that can be brought on by events as simple as a car travelling a long distance and building up an electric charge. Budden's theories have a scientific basis and Puddy's case is, arguably, the perfect proof. So perfect, in fact, that it forms the final pages of his book *Electric UFOs*.[2] Another scenario might suggest that some external intelligence really did contact Maureen Puddy on several occasions, taking control of her senses and trying to communicate with her. If so, it is hard to say why this choice was made and what useful purpose was served.[3]

"Cold!? Just Don't Ask."

The Hessdalen Valley, South East of Trondheim in Norway is remote, thinly populated and little known. The valley has been host to sightings of strange lights. There is some doubt about when the phenomena started but in 1981 the reports were regular and reliable and they continued long enough to allow a dedicated team of UFO investigators to establish a research project. Project Hessdalen went public in the summer of 1983. Active investigations started that year with a smattering of equipment and the project was fully equipped and running by 21 January 1984, by which point it had already gathered some incredible findings. The universities in Bergen and Oslo along with Norway's Defence Research Establishment provided equipment to monitor magnetic events, photographic gear including spectrum grating equipment designed to indicate the solidity of the objects, a radar tracking rig and a laser.

The events showed fluctuations with periods of high and low activity but the team gathered dozens of photographs and some other data that remains hard to explain. Within the first month they had two genuine revelations. The radar tracking equipment showed small objects moving frequently and the team were sometimes unable to spot these objects with the naked eye. On 31 January 1984 a lengthy series of radar recordings was made over a number of hours all indicating objects within sight of the Project Hessdalen caravan. Repeated observations by the researchers found nothing visible in the air. This pattern was repeated over the whole investigation but on many other occasions the radar tracks matched with sightings made by researchers and local residents.

Nine times the team pointed a laser at the lights, noting a change in the behaviour of a target on eight of these occasions. The most spectacular such event happened around 7.30 p.m. on 12 January 1984 when a laser was pointed at a light that was flashing regularly. When the laser hit the light it doubled the frequency of its flashes. When the team turned off the laser the light returned to the first sequence. The exercise was repeated four times, showing the same result each time.

Whatever the team were dealing with, it defied scientific logic. Results from the spectrum gratings on the cameras indicated the objects photographed were solid. Radar traces indicated that these solid objects could move at supersonic speeds without creating a sonic boom. Put bluntly, these objects showed properties fitting a solid and non-solid. On many occasions the team observed lights that changed colour and brightness. In some cases the lights simply faded out completely whilst under observation.

Two Hessdalen radar images were forwarded to an American organisation, Ground Saucer Watch (GSW), specialising in expert photographic analysis of UFO cases. Their reports have been the graveyard of many hopeful cases. Their analysis indicated that the Hessdalen radar images appeared to be from a good radar-reflecting source which was, apparently, more dense in the centre. Perhaps the most insightful comment they could offer was that "The return appears to be more indicative of one from a water-laden cloud."

In an echo of the events described from East Anglia and Tehran, the phenomena at Hessdalen appeared to be aware of the investigators. There were several strange equipment malfunctions, never properly explained. Some malfunctions continued after the equipment had been dismantled, investigated and checked for problems. On two consecutive nights lights appeared on radar within a minute of the videotape used to record the screen running to an end. On other occasions team members would arrive in their cars, be confronted with a sighting immediately and then go to the caravan for a night in which they would record nothing. One local resident once reported feeling the pressing urge to walk outside her house. When she did she saw a light passing by. All of this alleged intelligence shown by the lights could, of course, be nothing but coincidence.[4]

The Project Hessdalen team produced hard scientific data in the most extreme of conditions. The findings may be expressed in terms of scientific terminology but the reality was that there were a handful of dedicated researchers with borrowed equipment. The centre of investigations was a lonely caravan in which the research decisions involved the grim realities of unplugging heaters to free sockets for radar equipment. We're talking Nórway in January. I once asked Hessdalen founder member Odd-Gunnar Roed about the winter temperatures in the caravan. Considering he is one of the few UFOlogists in history who has been able to go to his investigations with real expectations of having his own experience Roed is remarkably laid-back. Ask him about those winter nights and he gets animated. "Cold!?" he sighed letting a slow resigned shrug of his shoulders speak volumes, "Just don't ask." The project, and the lights, have kept a low profile recently but new equipment and new reports were both arriving as this book went to press. Project Hessdalen has produced real UFO evidence. But, evidence for what?[5]

The researchers believed they were dealing with a strange atmospheric phenomenon. The ability of the objects to exhibit the properties of solid and non-solid objects suggests we may be looking at some form of plasma, a gaseous phenomena that might be able to assemble and disassemble in solid form. If so, how and why this occurs remains a mystery. The investigation of piezoelectricity, a process by which minerals and crystals under pressure produce electric fields, does show some

70

promise in this area. At great enough intensities these charges can ionise the air, producing light phenomena. This brings us back to the notions of earthlights discussed earlier and there is some evidence. Researcher Paul Devereux has done his own experiments to show that rocks crushed under pressure can produce light phenomena in the surrounding air. In 1986 Brian Grady and Glen Rowell, researchers at the US Bureau Of Mines, published a paper in the journal *Nature* discussing the short-lived light forms they had viewed in rock-crush experiments. The forms showed some similarities in behaviour to the Hessdalen observations. How these phenomena occur in laboratories and might occur in the atmosphere remains an area of complicated scientific debate.[6]

"You Bastard!"

I got a phone call at work one day from Justin Williams, a journalist on the local *Kent Messenger* who was researching material for a series called 'Kent's X-Files.' He'd heard me a few days earlier doing a local radio programme on UFOs and wanted to check out any leads I might have. A few days later we were sat either side of his desk at the *Kent Messenger*'s Larkfield base. One event I discussed with him was the Dargle Cottage case. An obscure number by UFO standards, but local to Kent. The case revolved around an elderly couple. Mr and Mrs Anthony Verney lived in a semi-remote Kent cottage in the late 1970s and early 1980s and claimed their lives were ruined by strange phenomena from a secret bunker nearby. Assuming the whole thing wasn't a paranoid delusion, the likeliest explanation is that a military bunker was being used for experiments with electronic equipment, possibly weaponry, designed to direct low frequency radiation. Anthony Verney wrote copiously to complain and demand action. His correspondence with then Prime Minister Margaret Thatcher is one rare case in which a private individual outdid her for assertiveness. The case, though long dead in terms of activity, still makes the UFO literature on two counts. Firstly, the possibility that electronic mind-control experiments could cause UFO-like events supports the theories of people like Albert Budden. Secondly, it appeals to those with a belief in conspiracies because the terse official replies look for all the world like blanket denials. Dargle Cottage makes a fleeting appearance in Robin Ramsay's Pocket Essential on *Conspir-*

acy Theories where the basis and context of the alleged experiments are explained.[7]

Justin said he'd look into it. Driving home from his office it struck me that I'd never written anything about the case myself. In that brief period when UFO magazines were littering the news-stands there would be money in an easy piece of writing. The following Saturday, 13 April 1996, with my wife away at her annual Psychotherapy Conference, I'd already promised to take our son Thom for a special treat. He was 3 and a half, loved Thomas The Tank Engine and wanted nothing more than a ride on the local Tenterden Steam Railway. We had a brilliant afternoon and Thom fell into a contented doze as we started the drive home. Dargle Cottage isn't visible from the road but the sign at the gate is clear, and located on a quiet road near Tenterden. The site of the alleged experiments is underground on farm land, now turned into a pitch-and-putt golf course. I could get pictures of both locations inside 15 minutes and still get home for the football results.

I was just getting the second shot when a car came round a corner on the tiny country road and passed slowly by. Driving away I saw the same car pulled to the side. When I drove past, it pulled out to follow me. The couple inside looked a little like Mulder and Scully. Young, smartly dressed and wearing shades. Not exactly normal for the Kent country-side on a Saturday afternoon. I drove to the main road, picked a lay-by and dived in at the last minute leaving them no time to follow me and no room to stop. I took their number, dropped back and followed them. A few miles later they were on my tail following a rapid reversal out of a farm road onto the main road. This was for real, my three-year-old son was fast asleep on the back seat and if I was going to be made to pay for stumbling onto a biggie I didn't want him in the firing line. We got to Maidstone and I lost them, turning late into a small series of back roads near my home. Even if they'd followed me I knew these roads well. I knew I had a chance to lose them. Mulder and Scully were nowhere in sight when I got home.

The following Monday I rang two people, a mate who could trace their car number and Justin Williams. "I really want to speak to you," he said, "There's still something happening at Dargle Cottage."

"Yeah, tell me about it," I said, launching into my experience. I'd hardly started when he let rip.

"You bastard!" he shouted.

72

The rest fell into place in seconds. He'd been driving the other car with his colleague Beth Mullins beside him as they did their research for 'Kent's X-Files.' Three days before we'd been no more than six feet apart for almost an hour, both of us agreeing that we had an interest in the subject but had a sceptical and pragmatic approach. The previous Saturday afternoon neither of us had recognised the other one. We'd gone further than that. I'd seen two people who didn't belong in that area and drawn a blank trying to reason it away as anything but some operation linked to Dargle Cottage.

Justin had even more evidence to scare him. He'd already run a check on my number plate and linked the car to the Kent County motor pool. A newish Rover saloon that belonged to the County. To him this meant one thing. As a journalist he knew that undercover police operations used cars just like this because they didn't look out of place anywhere. He also noticed the two security passes in the windscreen of my car, one for my college and one for my wife's workplace. He connected them with the place towards which I'd led him that afternoon. We'd come into Maidstone on a main road that brought us right past County Police Headquarters. The point at which I'd dived out into the country to lose them would have allowed me to do a simple diversion and get back to Police Headquarters within minutes. Justin had seen a man standing next to a lonely gate and looking directly at a location he knew to have some links with an unexplained case. The same bloke had got into a saloon car, spent time chasing him and Beth along two roads, and shown every sign of wanting to get back to Police Headquarters. Justin knew he'd stumbled into some trouble, until I rang him.

For a couple of clear thinking, intelligent sceptics we were a disgrace that afternoon. A few years later I can see this as a lucky break. It brought several things home to me. For starters, the things we saw were the things we expected to see once it was obvious there was a chase on. I didn't see, or consider I might be looking at, Justin. Frankly, I wasn't thinking beyond getting Thom out of harm's way. Justin didn't recognise me or see the child seat in the back of my undercover police car.

We were always going to sort it out because both of us desperately wanted to speak to the other the following Monday. But, there must be many other cases where people don't make such connections.

Outside of the world's official UFO tourist attractions, like the assorted attractions around Roswell, there are hundreds of unofficial locations. In the UK alone people stumble to places as remote as Rendlesham Forest, a mountain near Bala in Wales and the forest clearing in which Bob Taylor's trousers came to grief. They stop, look around, prod the ground and generally do things that others might consider suspicious. They want that proximity to a place where a UFO is supposed to have hit the ground. Rationally, they don't expect to find a thing. But these pilgrimages are not about being rational. They are about wanting contact with a mystery that remains elusive. I'm not having a go. I'm one of these people! I've been to the places described in books and Websites, looked and wondered. Sometimes, I've come to my own conclusions but I've never learned more than I did as a result of that April afternoon.

What I know from personal experience now is that your mindset at these moments is everything. Put yourself in a UFO-related location, suspect that the place might be under surveillance and you only need a couple of hydro-geologists in the area, dressed in coveralls and taking a soil sample to a Land Rover, to prove you were right about that UFO crash all along.

This chapter has highlighted things that matter greatly in the search for UFO answers and only the Maureen Puddy case contains a suggestion of anything alien. For UFOlogy to solve the big mysteries it has to take on board the complexities of all cases. It isn't easy to figure out what all of this might mean.

6. So What?

We have too many answers chasing too little evidence. As in politics, more people claim they have the answers than deliver progress.

There is progress being made in research. More importantly, there is a mystery here substantial enough to excite anyone with courage, a brain and determination. And UFOlogy is big. Big in its ideas, big in the range of answers on offer and big enough to reach the population of the whole planet. Someday, maybe, it will do more than that. It could provide us with answers about who we are and what we are doing here. It almost certainly will provide us with some answers about the world around us.

So what does it all mean? In the absence of proof you can draw your own conclusions. In the search for conclusions to this book we can do little better than line up the usual suspects and consider their claims.

Space Is The Place

Many people believe that UFOs come from space, although the exact place(s) in space are still argued over. Some of the evidence doesn't pass muster in any scientific sense. Religious groups, like The Aetherius Society, who claim contact with inhabitants of our own Solar System living in higher spiritual realms, are certainly out on their own. Scientifically, their claims are possible only in terms of discoveries as yet unmade. They have a crude logic but also a raft of detractors within both UFOlogy and science. On the other hand, there are cases of channelled contacts, telepathic messages and the bizarre array of alien forms who arrive with messages and/or a purpose to their mission. Hard evidence or not, there is a pattern to many UFO reports that indicates some intelligence trying to reach us.

It is notable that in case after case the witnesses don't seem to question the extraterrestrial origins of the beings they meet. Antonio Villas Boas made love to a being who was certainly humanoid and indicated that she would give birth to his child in space. Maureen Puddy instinctively knew she was dealing with a spaceman.

In terms of the harder evidence there are claims about planets of origin. Some, like the many abductees in the last two decades who seem to meet Grey aliens, have a consistency. Some claims, based on everything from information gathered at hypnotic regression sessions to alleged leaks of classified information, pinpoint the origins. In recent years, Zeta Reticuli has become a particular favourite. The hard evidence for this eludes us. The history of 'definitive proof' in this area is the history of evidence that failed to appear or disappointed when it did.

Probably the strongest case in this regard is still the Dogon tribe and their belief about the Nommos from Sirius. Whatever the truth about that case it does have elements that mark it out as more than mass hysteria. Also, there is certainly a lot of suspect evidence in the world of ancient astronauts but this field is kept alive by the enduring mystery about ourselves and the origins of our civilisation. There are gaps in all the arguments and the evidence supporting these arguments. It is too simplistic to state without real evidence that aliens intervened and created us in their own image. But there are cases, like the Piri Re'is map and the Book Of Ezekiel, that offer some substance with that supposition.

The strongest argument against the ExtraTerrestrial Hypotheses (ETH) is the consistent lack of proof and the consistent disintegration of the cases that offered the proof. But claims and mysteries remain and some cases, like the incidents at Bentwaters and Tehran, do present hard evidence and unmistakable encounters with something beyond our comprehension. More importantly in terms of the ETH, they show objects that appear to possess physical capabilities and intelligence, or intelligent control, beyond the level of our own. If, as Ralph Noyes claimed, the MOD ruled out alien origin for such phenomena they must know something significant that has never been made public. If not, we are a long way short of proving alien intervention on our own planet, but it remains a possibility.

The God Slot

UFOlogy is a religion. That is fact. From the organisations registered as religious charities to the ceremonies that see massed Aetherians chanting on holy mountains like Holdstone Down in Devon, there are religions based around UFO belief. Pragmatic and cynical demolitions of such groups exist but most of these groups contain self-aware people, content with their lot. Marshall Applewhite and his Heaven's Gate suicide commandos, who committed communal Hari Kari as the Hale Bopp comet passed the Earth, are very much the exception in this company.

More debatable is the notion that UFOlogy and the UFO community are a pseudo religious movement. Some outsiders, especially those who make the study of society their business, say yes. But they'd be eaten alive, metaphorically speaking, by the people they are describing in these claims. Whatever the views of those inside the UFO community, it's true that the issues and ideas that draw some of them in can act as a surrogate religion. Anecdotally the evidence is there, in the way some pieces of evidence are treated as important relics and the way that faith upholds some stories in the absence of proof. Many stories, for example some of the crash retrievals, are completely an item of faith. The miracle cures for AIDS and colour-blindness are believed by some in the UFO community, but are unsupported by medical science. As we saw in the last chapter, some of the roots of the crash retrieval stories may be government disinformation. John A Saliba wrote a paper outlining the fact that UFO stories present a range of classic religious ideas: mystery; transcendence; the existence of supernatural entities; images of perfection; ideas of salvation; a world-view that appeals; and an explanation of spirituality.[1] Look through the stories in this book and these themes will emerge. Directly in the case of Ezekiel being given a vision. Indirectly in the contact between Maureen Puddy and her spaceman.

The existence of the supernatural and, by implication, another realm that would appear miraculous and perfect to many on Earth, is implicit in the stories of beings who can float humans through walls and windows into waiting spacecraft. Belief in such stories can bind people to UFO groups. To say UFOlogy is a religion or pseudo religion is probably an overstatement but belief in UFOs does address needs that may also be met by religious teachings. UFO belief continues to rise in a period that has seen the major established religions fragmenting. In an era that has seen a satirical church devoted to The Partridge Family[2] and the serious discussion of religious experiences involving the spirit of Elvis Presley, the notion of the space brothers acting as guardian angels isn't so unusual.

The Appliance Of Science

UFOlogy is not a recognised science. Not a physical science and not a social science. Many investigators in groups and their counterparts in professional science are openly hostile to each other. Still, UFOs have provided some small scientific breakthroughs. The earthlight theories go hand in hand with research in tectonics and geology. The ideas about electromagnetic hypersensitivity promoted by a handful of researchers are also founded on observation. Michael Persinger and Albert Budden haven't proven the causes of abduction beyond reasonable doubt but they do have workable models that are showing progress.

Project Hessdalen, the radar-visual cases that have gathered evidence of aerial lightforms and encounters like the one involving Stefan Michalak, has produced hard evidence. UFOlogy may not be any kind of recognised science but the evidence of these cases can be of use to recognised sciences.

It won't please many directly within the UFO community but it may well be that some of the key scientific breakthroughs that solve UFO mysteries will come from unrelated studies. For example, the work suggesting that electromagnetic pollution may be a key cause of abductions could have other uses. Researchers in this field do not generally claim that abduction events are the only psychological effects to result from such pollution. One sector of commerce who may eventually take a stronger interest in this work is the insurance industry. If mobile phone masts, cars with badly insulated electronics and television transmitters really are a threat to our sanity then the telecommunications industry could face massive claims like those currently being unleashed on the tobacco industry. UFO research could be crucial to the claims. One or two in the UFO world might resent the hijacking of their work and the conclusions drawn but the simple fact is that the insurance industry has the financial muscle to sustain a campaign like this. At the moment the evidence that suggests it would be worthwhile is thin on the ground but there is some evidence to suggest that abduction cases resemble stories of kidnap by fairies in the past. There are also other puzzling events, like Albert Burtoo's encounter, that produce sincere witnesses and stories that seem to be part logic and part nonsense. In a word, dreamlike. This notion is further supported by the controversial study carried out by Lawson and McCall that at least hinted that we may all be able to produce abduction experiences, even when others know for sure that no abduction took place.

One reason that so many abduction stories are believed to involve extraterrestrials is that those doing the research often believe this to be the case. If a third party, like the insurance industry, were to finance a massive study looking for other evidence, like an increase in psychotic episodes after the erection of a new television transmitter near a city, they might find the records of the local UFO group to be a gold mine.

We're a long way from that day. If it ever came it is likely that the UFO researchers surrendering evidence would be almost as miserable as those in the dock. How would you expect them to feel watching their evidence being used to prove that extraterrestrial messages received by a schoolboy were nothing more than an undiagnosed epileptic episode caused by the careless activities of a television company?

Ironically, science and UFOlogy are furthest apart where their interests are most common - in the search for proof of extraterrestrial life. Consider the roles of those employed in SETI-related work and UFOlogists and this makes sense. Each side often considers the other engaged in pointless work with no reason to exist. To many UFOlogists the radio telescopes trained into infinity are a waste of money when there are landing sites at Rendlesham Forest, Roswell and the rest that might yield better evidence. There is a certain ironic comedy in this situation if only because the other common ground that UFOlogy and SETI share is a history of throwing huge efforts into searches that produce interesting and marginally useful results. The big prize continues to elude both sides.

But this prolonged animosity is not the whole picture. There are a handful of researchers on either side moving easily between both areas and there are also periodic attempts to combine forces. In the case of abductions the Massachusetts Institute Of Technology hosted a high-powered symposium in 1992, recorded in CDB Bryan's *Close Encounters Of The Fourth Kind*, that brought the leaders of abduction research face to face with social scientists and a smattering of other interested parties. There were some volatile eruptions, especially when those in the UFO community began discussing the research methods that allowed them to estimate the number of people being abducted. But there was progress and understanding too.

Occasionally, physical science and UFOlogy have also combined to useful effect. At the end of June 1998 a nine-member panel of scientists under the direction of Peter Sturrock, a physicist from Stanford University, California, reported on a project examining UFO reports. Their findings, although expressed in a more positive tone, resembled the reports of official US government investigations of the past. They also correlated broadly with the conclusions drawn in France by GEPAN/SEPRA. The panel found anomalies and genuine mysteries in the UFO data but it found little to indicate that there was evidence of extraterrestrial visitation.

There is no doubt that social and physical science can help those involved in UFO research to make progress. There is also no doubt that evidence gathered in the course of UFO investigation could help researchers in the sciences. In the physical sciences phenomena like ball lightning remain mysterious. In social science, conditions like Fantasy Prone Personality Disorder remain to be quantified and fully understood. The hard evidence collected by UFOlogists may be useful to these sciences. For UFO researchers genuinely interested in solving cases, the occasional chance to work directly with professionals is a bonus. It is probably, also, the best chance for the subject of UFOlogy to gain credibility and respect.

You Don't Have To Be Mad To Work Here

Linked to the social scientific investigations into UFOs is the central question of whether any of the experiences described can be explained by psychology. We're long past dismissing the whole thing as madness but we cannot say that all experiences described are genuine, physical encounters. The major problems to being definite either way are a lack of evidence on the clinical side and a confusion of evidence in the area of UFO experience. One thing we can safely say is that no one trigger experience brings about UFO events. In some cases people simply misidentify things: Meteors, the planet Venus and aircraft regularly prompt UFO reports. The people making the reports generally make them in all sincerity but UFO researchers are often wise to the patterns of certain types of misidentifications. Jenny Randles told me that if an event of an airborne object exceeds 5 minutes then, as a rule, it pays to look for an astronomical solution.

The misidentifications go to the heart of the business. The Kenneth Arnold sighting that started the modern era of UFOlogy may well have been a misidentification. At one end of the psychological spectrum we have simple slips of identification. At the other we are dealing with full-blown altered states of consciousness serious enough to take over some-one's life. There are contradictions in the messages channelled and gathered directly from aliens. This proves, at least, that some channelled contacts and direct encounters with aliens are not what they seem. This leaves us with the problem of explaining the causes of such messages. It is likely that the future will show developments in understanding psychological conditions that will advance both clinical practice and the understanding of UFO experience.

The major reason we cannot reach conclusions at the present time is because we lack definitive diagnostic tools for conditions like Fantasy Prone Personality Disorder (FPP). Most of the conditions that might explain UFO encounters are either the stuff of peer-reviewed journals or established within areas of clinical practice that don't generally bring the practitioners into contact with UFO investigation. FPP is firmly within the former category. It is not presented in the *DSM* (Diagnostic and Statistical Manual) series of books, which are the definitive diagnostic tools for clinical practice. FPP is an item of debate and discussion amongst some therapists attempting to understand patients. As more work is done to understand this condition, it is likely that FPP will eventually appear as a diagnosable clinical condition. If it doesn't, then like Gulf War Syndrome, it is likely that research based around consistently observed behaviour will still have deepened our understanding.

Some established conditions may provide insights into existing UFO cases. Lynn Picknett's *Mammoth Book Of UFOs* considered a visual disorder, Charles Bonnet Syndrome (CBS), as a potential basis for explaining sightings of beings or craft that were not seen by others. As explanations for UFO events go CBS is an outsider at present. CBS is a visual disorder that affects the elderly and is only found in patients who have suffered damage to their sight. You could not diagnose, for example, Maureen Puddy's encounter in this way. She was 37 at the time of the main event described in this book and able to see well. However, CBS does establish beyond doubt that sane elderly people with damaged eyes can see things that are not there and they often perceive the hallucinatory visions for what they are. It also establishes that the relationship between the nervous system controlling our eyes and the centres of the brain concerned with the creation of meaning is complex. CBS won't explain Maureen Puddy, Alfred Burtoo, Joe Simonton or the many other encounters with craft and occupants presenting vivid experiences for the witness and little or no corroboration from others. However, it may be that in the clinical literature on conditions like CBS there are nuggets of information that will eventually lead to such an understanding. This and other conditions, for example Temporal Lobe Epilepsy, are still being investigated by medical science.

Ongoing investigations need evidence. Psychological investigations usually start with a hard core of cases in which a compelling core of evidence presents researchers with the basis for diagnosing a condition. At this point understanding the condition depends on exploring a larger body of evidence. For this reason, it is likely that many of the major breakthroughs in UFO investigation will come from neuro-science and psychology. This will happen because there will be time and money for research. In some cases those doing the research will see the sense, as Dr Michael Persinger does, in using UFO accounts and claimants as the basis for investigation. Such work will happen but it is impossible to predict where it will take us.

The Infotainment Scam

It's likely you bought this book or borrowed it from someone who paid for it. This book exists because Pocket Essentials saw the financial sense in adding a title to their range of punchy and informative works on everything from *Joel & Ethan Coen* to *Conspiracy Theories*. I, as the author, have been aware of the UFO market for years. I've wanted to write a UFO book like this for a long time but I had a problem. The books that sell millions of copies are the ones that claim that the aliens are here and coming for us all, and I was never likely to write a book like that. If I self-published or went through a small, anonymous publishing house, then the sales reps would have been politely, but firmly, told, "Not interested." Pocket Essentials on the other hand have a house style, a track record of no-nonsense writing and a presence in the major bookshop chains.

This matters because it is the most pertinent example I can show you of the value of UFO information. The information in this book had a value before the book existed. Its value to the publisher is proven because they invested money and commissioned the title. Pocket Essentials are not short of subject ideas or potential writers. Their survival depends on making profitable decisions from these options. If I wanted to make money as an author I was always going to be better off putting my work with a company who have distribution organised, a track record of selling books and an established style and market.

Work outwards from this example and we find a key point of UFOlogy. Outside of direct research into events, or more accurately, reports of events, the information we gather is usually produced commercially. Academic research may be one exception to this rule but most of the academic papers UFOlogists own on their subject are compiled in commercially available books. The Internet has changed this in recent years.

The market for UFO information has consistently liked work claiming aliens are real, governments cover things up and the proof of both of these claims is in the book/magazine/Website/video you are about to buy. This is a situation that has cast UFOs and aliens as a potent market force. More importantly, this situation has ensured an abundance of pro-extraterrestrial material at the expense of other views. In cases like Roswell the various views exist in print, partly, because the name recognition alone is a market winner.

One obvious effect of this situation is to ensure that the definitive truth will, almost certainly, never be known. There are precedents for this. For example, the death of Marilyn Monroe and the identity of Jack The Ripper remain shrouded in mystery partly because the subjects have shown themselves to be consistently lucrative as media source material. Much material sells on the basis of a revision or new angle. Like the Roswell case, the only realistic hope of an end to the speculation is the emergence of a new piece of definitive evidence. This is an unlikely prospect in all these cases.

The market-led nature of UFO information is killing the search for the truth. Often an adherence to the truth and an awareness of market needs make an uneasy alliance. Remember the point that Timothy Good made in his *Guardian* interview promoting the massive-selling *Beyond Top Secret*: "If ever there's a subject that needs rescuing from its supporters, it's this one."

The popularity of UFOs and aliens as a subject has a direct bearing on the way the subject is understood. Timothy Good's massive book sales are only one aspect of this popularity. During the mid- to late-1990s, it was widely claimed that surfing on the Internet for UFOs, the paranormal and conspiracy theories was second only to sex in popularity. The world's most popular television series and films are based on the assumption that aliens exist. For over twenty years *Star Trek* was widely acknowledged as the most popular and lucrative TV series ever made. Today, depending on which set of statistics you believe, the most successful television series is either *Star Trek*, *The X-Files* or *The Simpsons*. The premise of *Star Trek* is that mankind will explore space in the future the way we explored this planet in the past. So we will encounter life, but not necessarily as we know it, as we explore. The premise of *The X-Files* is that many paranormal events are based on realities we don't yet comprehend and that secret branches of government conspire to cover up this information. *The Simpsons* is different but this animated sitcom has featured aliens and alien-related plot events. It has also paid homage to high-profile science fiction, especially *Star Wars*.

The point, I hope, is made. UFO and alien ideas are widely understood, potentially profitable and adaptable over time. This matters because one theme running through nearly all of the cases outlined in this book is that many people encountering aliens, apparently for real, are also confronted with a reality that makes a general kind of sense. In most cases aliens appear to be ahead of us in terms of technology and also have an awareness of the problems faced by the human race. This picture is, more or less, true even when the encounters don't involve space aliens. The American airship wave of the late nineteenth century included James Hooten's meeting with an airship captain who used "compressed air and aeroplanes."

The whole airship wave was, almost certainly, fiction. However, the audience didn't always think so. The 1950s contactees similarly had a large following who believed every word. Today aliens impart a different wisdom or carry out interbreeding programmes, possibly to benefit mankind and themselves. In every generation we appear to have some kind of archetypal story of encountering other realms and realities. In the media age we have an access to information on an unprecedented scale and almost everything can be accessed, literally, at the speed of light.

The expectations of audiences certainly influence the material they choose to read, watch and surf. The question of how far our expectations in each generation have influenced UFO reports is harder to answer.

So Farewell Then

This subject doesn't have the closure of other Pocket Essentials subjects. There are virtually no formulae or rules to memorise that will make you an instant UFO expert. The more you look for answers the more you find questions. UFOlogy is puzzling, downright frightening, frequently hilarious and always capable of surprising you.

I've learned some survival strategies over the years. Confronted with someone who claims to have the hard evidence in the definitive case I'm no longer impressed. When I hear another variation on the cover-up and conspiracy stories I am, once again, inclined to cynicism. But it is an odd kind of disbelief because I'd love to be wrong. In fact, if some major political figure throws open the hangar doors and shows us all the anti-matter reactor that arrived with the alien craft, I'd be happy to have got it wrong over the years.

As I wrote at the start, this is a subject that offers people a lifetime of lateral thinking. It is also a subject that allows an amateur to make a major contribution. So, if you're lacking that sense of closure and still wondering what happened at Roswell or over the Bass Strait, there is one solution open to you: get involved.

Notes

Books, Websites, articles and live presentations pillage the same cases. In the best-known cases, like Roswell, the sources quoted here are chosen because, in the opinion of this author, they present an accessible and authoritative way to follow up the introduction provided by this book.

1. Introduction

1. Leonard Stringfield, 'The Search For Proof In A Squirrel's Cage' in Hilary Evans & John Spencer, *UFOs 1947-1987 The 40 Year Search For An Explanation*, Fortean Tomes 1987, pp 145-155.
2. Joseph Allen Hynek (1910-1986) arguably did for UFO studies what Elvis Presley did for popular music. A scientist with a PhD in Astrophysics who first became involved in the subject via official investigations, Hynek was initially of a sceptical persuasion and - briefly - became a figure of some vilification when the press and public were unconvinced by his assertion that a series of UFO events in Michigan may have been caused by swamp gas igniting. It was unfair on a man whose allegiance to the "Hippocratic oath of a scientist" meant he pursued truth above anything else. This led Hynek to write *The UFO Experience* (1972), *The Edge Of Reality* (1975) and *The Hynek UFO Report* (1977). In these books he stated his view that UFOs represented a compelling and substantial challenge to established scientific thought. In an area troubled, then as now, with sensational writing and sketchy research, Hynek's work allowed the subject to raise itself towards respectability.
3. *The Armchair UFOlogist* remains the quintessential cult item in the field not least because it is not open for subscription. If you're happening, the journal will find you. I can't improve on Jenny Randles' description of Roberts in *The Little Giant UFO Encyclopaedia* as an 'irreverent wit and rational UFO investigator.'
4. James Oberg, 'The Failure Of The Science Of UFOlogy,' *New Scientist* 11 Oct 1979, pp 102-106.
5. Neil Nixon, 'UFOlogy - A Qualified Success?,' ed. Steve Moore, *Fortean Studies* 5, John Brown Publications 1998, pp 96-121.
6. Erich Von Daniken, *Chariots Of The Gods,* Souvenir 1969. Von Daniken remains the best selling and best known of a slew of authors who have popularised this branch of UFO investigation.
7. Josef F Blumrich, *The Spaceships Of Ezekiel,* Corgi 1974.

8. Carl Sagan (1934-1997) was another hugely influential thinker and investigator in the field.

9. The classics of which include John Michell's *The Flying Saucer Vision* (1967) and *The View Over Atlantis* (1969), and Ronald Story's *The Space Gods Revealed* (1976).

10. Robert Temple, *The Sirius Mystery,* Futura 1976.

11. David Barclay, *Aliens The Final Answer?*, Blandford 1995.

12. Drop yourself in at the deep end at http://home.talkcity.com/SpiritCir/gracewatcher/humanorigin.html.

13. Dr David Clarke, 'Once Upon A Time In The West,' Chapter 1 of *The UFOs That Never Were,* Jenny Randles, Andy Roberts & David Clarke, London House 2000, pp 15-32.

14. Jacques Vallee, *Challenge To Science,* Neville Spearman 1966 and *Passport To Magonia,* Neville Spearman 1970.

15. Jacques Vallee, *Passport To Magonia,* Neville Spearman 1970, pp 23-25.

16. David Barclay, *Aliens The Final Answer?*, Blandford 1995, pp 82-83.

17. James Easton, 'Flight Of Fantasy,' *Fortean Times* 137.

18. Hilary Evans & Dennis Stacy, *The UFO Mystery,* John Brown Publications 1998, pp 28-29.

19. Tim Shawcross, *The Roswell File,* Bloomsbury 1997, pp 143-144.

20. Ed David C Knight, *UFOs: A Pictorial History From Antiquity To The Present,* McGraw-Hill 1979, pp 31-33.

21. Jenny Randles & Peter Hough, *The Complete Book Of UFOs,* Piatkus 1994, pp 122-129.

22. A potted overview of the case appears in Alan Baker, *The Encyclopaedia Of Alien Encounters,* Virgin 1999, pp 19-20.

23. Curtis Peebles, *Watch The Skies: A Chronicle Of The Flying Saucer Myth,* Berkley Books 1995, pp 198-199.

24. Jenny Randles, *Aliens, The Real Story,* Hale 1993, p 29.

2. The Evidence For Alien Invaders

1. Timothy Good, *Above Top Secret,* Sidgwick and Jackson 1987, and *Beyond Top Secret,* Sidgwick and Jackson 1996.

2. Relax, it didn't.

3. Timothy Good, *Alien Liaison,* Arrow 1992. Lazar's claims are a major part of this book, the hard evidence of the payslip is on page 178.

4. John E Mack, *Abduction,* Simon and Schuster 1994, pp 41-43.

5. Jenny Randles, *UFO Retrievals,* Blandford 1995, pp 18-25. The whole book comes highly recommended as the best and most accessible collection of UFO crash stories.

6. Jenny Randles, Andy Roberts & David Clarke, *The UFOs That Never Were,* London House 2000, pp 196-197.

7. Jenny Randles, *Something In The Air,* Hale 1998, pp 124-131.

8. Edward Ashpole, *The UFO Phenomena,* Headline 1995, pp 116-125.

9. CDB Bryan, *Close Encounters Of The Fourth Kind,* Weidenfeld and Nicholson 1995, pp 19-20 & 26.

10. Jenny Randles, *Aliens, The Real Story,* Hale 1993, pp 61-63.

3. The UFO Community

1. Robert Durant, 'Public Opinion Polls And UFOs' in Hilary Evans & Dennis Stacy, *The UFO Mystery,* John Brown Publications 1998, pp 338-352.

2. Ken Phillips, 'The Anamnesis Report,' *Proceedings Of The 6th International UFO Congress*, pp 59-63.

3. Ken Phillips, 'The Psycho-Sociology Of UFOs,' ed. David Barclay, *UFOs, The Final Answer*, Blandford 1993, pp 40-64.

4. Judy O Parnell & R Leo Sprinkle, 'Personality Characteristics Of Persons Who Claim UFO Experiences,' *Journal Of UFO Studies* Vol 2, CUFOS 1990, pp 54-58.

5. SC Wilson & TX Barber, 'Vivid Fantasy And Hallucinatory Abilities In The Life Histories Of Excellent Hypnotic Subjects,' ed. E Klinger, *Imagery Volume 2, Concepts, Results, and Applications,* Plenum Press 1981.

6. Robert E Bartholomew & George S Howard, *UFOs And Alien Contact,* Prometheus Books 1998, pp 248-273.

7. Chris Rutkowski, *Abductions And Aliens,* Fusion Press 2000, pp 162-163.

8. Steven P Resta, *The Relationship Of Anomie And Externality To Strength Of Belief In Unidentified Flying Objects,* Masters dissertation, Loyola College Graduate School, Baltimore 1975.

9. Martin Kottmeyer, 'UFOlogy As An Evolving System Of Paranoia,' *UFO Conspiracy Theories* Vol 7, No. 3 May/June 1992, pp 28-35.

10. David Morris, *The Masks Of Lucifer,* Batsford 1990.

11. Vance Packard, *The Status Seekers,* Penguin 1963, p 44.

12. Dr R Leo Sprinkle, *Soul Samples,* Granite Publishing 1999.

13. Devereux and Budden have both written a series of books charting stages of their evolving studies. The most recent titles are, therefore, recommended. Probably the most accessible view into a radical take on many UFO events is Albert Budden's *Electric UFOs,* Blandford 1998.

14. Edward Ashpole, *The UFO Phenomena,* Headline 1995.

15. Jenny Randles, *Star Children,* Hale 1994, pp 161-182 provides an insightful discussion on UFO states of mind.

16. See the Pocket Essential *Conspiracy Theories*, p 55. The book also contains material on UFO conspiracies. RE Bartholomew's 'The Social Psychology Of 'Epidemic' Koro' appears in *International Journal Of Social Psychiatry* 40, no.1 1994, pp 46-60.

4. Amazing Tales

1. For a short introduction to the complexities try Tim Shawcross, *The Roswell File*, Bloomsbury 1997, which is a succinct and engaging consideration of the pro-UFO case. Lynn Picknett's *Mammoth Book Of UFOs*, Robinson 2001, contains a 59-page chapter entitled 'The Truth About The Roswell Incident' that is a triumph of concentration, managing to include the key details, a sense of balance and, ultimately, a demolition of anything other than earthbound explanations.

2. The Bentwaters case is a well-trodden event in UFO history. Jenny Randles, for one, has revisited the case several times. Martin Lawrence Shough's chapter, 'Distant Contact: Radar/Visual Encounter At Bentwaters,' eds. John Spencer & Hilary Evans, *Phenomenon*, Futura 1988, lacks some of Randles' recent forays into official documents but does provide one of the most vivid and authoritative tellings of the tale.

3. Jenny Randles, *Something In The Air*, Robert Hale 1998, pp 95-97.

4. Peter Hough & Moyshe Kalman, *The Truth About Alien Abductions*, Blandford 1997, pp 8-18.

5. Jenny Randles, *Something In The Air*, Robert Hale 1998, pp 139-144.

6. Timothy Good, *Beyond Top Secret,* Sidgewick And Jackson 1996, pp 87-93.

7. Abductions form a major part of the UFO literature and anyone interested in catching up on the classic accounts is recommended to investigate the work of Budd Hopkins and his Intruders Foundation. Hopkins' books, especially *Intruders*, Sphere 1987, remain classics in this area. Also worth hunting down are: David Jacobs' work, especially *Alien Encounters*, Virgin 1992; Dr John Mack's *Abduction*, Simon and Schuster 1994; and CDB Bryan's *Close Encounters Of The Fourth Kind*, Weidenfeld and Nicholson 1995. The latter is an account by a previously sceptical journalist of his attendance at an abduction conference and subsequent meetings with some of the main players.

5. Cautionary Tales

1. Story from William L Moore's article 'The Crown Of St Stephen And Crashed UFOs: The Oldest UFO Disinformation Case On Record,' *Far Out* Vol 1, No. 1 July 1992, pp 32-33. For a thorough round-up of crash retrieval stories see Jenny Randles, *UFO Retrievals: The Recovery Of Alien Spacecraft,* Blandford 1995.
2. Albert Budden, *Electric UFOs*, Blandford 1998, pp 262-8.
3. CDB Bryan, *Close Encounters Of The Fourth Kind*, Weidenfeld and Nicholson 1995, pp 70-75 covers the presentation of Puddy's case at the international symposium held at the Massachusetts Institute of Technology in 1992.
4. Odd-Gunnar Roed, 'Project Hessdalen,' *6th International Congress, UFOs: The Global View,* BUFORA/IUN 1991, pp 55-58.
5. David Clarke & Andy Roberts, *Phantoms Of The Sky,* Robert Hale 1990, pp 145-146.
6. Jim Schnabel, *Dark White*, Hamish Hamilton 1994, pp 125-126.
7. Robin Ramsay, *Conspiracy Theories*, Pocket Essentials 2000, p 78 places this event in a worldwide operation to test mind-control technology.

6. So What?

1. John A Saliba, 'Religious Dimensions Of The UFO Abductee Experience,' ed. James R Lewis, *The Gods Have Landed*, State University Of New York Press 1995, pp 15-64.
2. Headed by the Most Reverend Point Me In The Direction Of Albuquerque Partridge.

Glossary

Abduction - A claimed event in which humans or animals are removed from their normal surroundings to a UFO generally for the purposes of investigation or instruction.

Abductee - Someone who has been abducted, see above.

Case - A generic term for a UFO or UFO-related event. Cases are often identified by their locale, (Roswell), or the name of the witness(es), (Cash/Landrum). The apportioning of such names and the decision on whether one event or a series form a case is somewhat informal.

Crash Retrieval - The recovery of debris following the alleged UFO crash.

ETH - The ExtraTerrestrial Hypothesis. The belief in extraterrestrial life and its interaction with life on Earth. A staple assumption of much UFOlogical thought.

Flap - A period of intense UFO-related activity centred on a particular place. Flaps come and go and are, therefore, not to be confused with so-called window areas in which UFOs are consistently reported.

FPP - Fantasy Prone Personality. Theory suggesting susceptibility to fantasy experiences. Advanced in 1981 since when it has remained a controversial aspect to some explanations of UFO experience.

Grey - Generic term for small alien with spindly body and large eyes. Grey reports show some variation although the image of the grey is now widely recognised within society as a whole.

Implant - An object forcibly placed inside the subject of an abduction. The purpose of the alleged implants is a matter of debate. One common belief claims them as tracking devices.

Radar-Visual – Sometimes radar/visual. A sighting in which a witness sighting of a UFO or UFOs is supported by radar evidence indicating a positive return for the object(s) sighted.

SETI - Search for ExtraTerrestrial Intelligence. An organised scientific operation with headquarters in California. The group search for extraterrestrial life using radio astronomy from sites around the world.

UFO - Unidentified Flying Object. In reality a term used to describe any unexplained phenomena seen in the sky and, in some cases, the observation of strange objects on land or sea that may conceivably fly.

UFOlogist - One who studies UFOs. More properly, one who studies reports of UFO events either by means of direct involvement in chasing up reports or copious consumption of UFO literature allied to critical thinking.

Window Area - A place in which UFO events are regularly reported.

Websites

UFOs haunt the Internet. UFOs have found a welcoming environment in a realm that allows virtually unlimited imaginative freedom and offers the chance that anyone, regardless of the extremity of their beliefs, will find a kindred spirit. The following sites are a tiny fraction of the material on offer. Each is selected because it offers an insight into some aspect of the mystery and further links for the curious.

Paranormal Resources Primer - www.tje.net/para/main - A substantial introduction with explanations, links and well-presented exemplar material. Not limited to UFOs but a good introduction to them as a subject in a wider context. Like the majority of detailed Websites, based in the USA.

www.ufoinfo.com – UK-based site offering regular updates, substantial amounts of information and a pragmatic introduction to all things UFO. Intolerant of the extreme cults and ideas. Otherwise, open-minded and user-friendly.

www.ufoin.org.uk - More lateral thinking and intelligent than many sites. Based around the questing and questioning approach of the UK's more open-minded researchers. A good place to visit for a well-reasoned alternative to the more hysterical and populist arguments.

Intruders Foundation - www.intrudersfoundation.org - The best-known organisation in the area of investigation into alien abductions. User-friendly, open about its beliefs and headed by Budd Hopkins, a leader in this field.

www.xdream.freeserve.co.uk/homepage - One example of how strange it can get. 'Alien life forms influence rock music and popular culture' and Daniel Transit tells it like it is. Charting the role of the rock music industry as a front organisation for the alien presence on Earth and revealing just what the work of Kate Bush, Elvis and David Bowie may really be about. Liberally linked to other sites. Frankly, I have doubts about the truth of the claims but the site is accessible, user-friendly and likely to fire your awareness and imagination.

The Essential Library

Conspiracy Theories by Robin Ramsay, £3.99

Do you think the X-Files is fiction? That Elvis is dead? That the US actually went to the moon? And don't know that the ruling elite did a deal with the extra-terrestrials after the Roswell crash in 1947... At one time, you could blame the world's troubles on the Masons or the Illuminati, or the Jews, or One Worlders, or the Great Communist Conspiracy. Now we also have the alien-US elite conspiracy, or the alien shape-shifting reptile conspiracy to worry about - and there are books to prove it as well! This book tries to sort out the handful of wheat from the choking clouds of intellectual chaff. For among the nonsensical Conspiracy Theory rubbish currently proliferating on the Internet, there are important nuggets of real research about real conspiracies waiting to be mined.

Ancient Greece by Mike Paine, £3.99

Western civilization began with the Greeks. From the highpoint of the 5th century BC through the cultural triumphs of the Alexandrian era to their impact on the developing Roman empire, the Greeks shaped the philosophy, art, architecture and literature of the Mediterranean world. Mike Paine provides a concise and well-informed narrative of many centuries of Greek history. He highlights the careers of great political and military leaders like Pericles and Alexander the Great, and shows the importance of the great philosophers like Plato and Aristotle. Dramatists and demagogues, stoics and epicureans, aristocrats and helots take their places in the unfolding story of the Greek achievement.

Black Death by Sean Martin, £3.99

The Black Death is the name most commonly given to the pandemic of bubonic plague that ravaged the medieval world in the late 1340s. From Central Asia the plague swept through Europe, leaving millions of dead in its wake. Between a quarter and a third of Europe's population died. In England the population fell from nearly six million to just over three million. The Black Death was the greatest demographic disaster in European history.

The Essential Library

The Crusades by Mike Paine, £3.99

The first crusade was set in motion by Pope Urban II in 1095 and culminated in the capture of Jerusalem from the Muslims four years later. In 1291 the fall of Acre marked the loss of the last Christian enclave in the Holy Land. This Pocket Essential traces the chronology of the Crusades between these two dates and highlights the most important figures on all sides of the conflict.

Alchemy & Alchemists by Sean Martin, £3.99

Alchemy is often seen as an example of medieval gullibility and the alchemists as a collection of eccentrics and superstitious fools. Sean Martin shows that nothing could be further from the truth. It is important to see the search for the philosopher's stone and the attempts to turn base metal into gold as metaphors for the relation of man to nature and man to God as much as seriously held beliefs. Alchemists like Paracelsus and Albertus Magnus were amongst the greatest minds of their time. This book traces the history of alchemy from ancient times to the 20th century, highlighting the interest of modern thinkers like Jung in the subject.

American Civil War by Phil Davies, £3.99

The American Civil War, fought between North and South in the years 1861-1865, was the bloodiest and most traumatic war in American history. Rival visions of the future of the United States faced one another across the battlefields and families and friends were bitterly divided by the conflict. This book examines the deep-rooted causes of the war, so much more complicated than the simple issue of slavery.

American Indian Wars by Howard Hughes, £3.99

At the beginning of the 1840s the proud tribes of the North American Indians looked across the plains at the seemingly unstoppable expansion of the white man's West. During the decades of conflict that followed, as the new world pushed onward, the Indians saw their way of life disappear before their eyes. Over the next 40 years they clung to a dream of freedom and a continuation of their traditions, a dream that was repeatedly shattered by the whites.

The Essential Library: Currently Available

Film Directors:

Woody Allen (Revised)	Tim Burton	Ang Lee
Jane Campion*	John Carpenter	Steve Soderbergh
Jackie Chan	Joel & Ethan Coen	Clint Eastwood
David Cronenberg	Terry Gilliam*	Michael Mann
Alfred Hitchcock	Krzysztof Kieslowski*	
Stanley Kubrick	Sergio Leone	
David Lynch	Brian De Palma*	
Sam Peckinpah*	Ridley Scott	
Orson Welles	Billy Wilder	
Steven Spielberg	Mike Hodges	

Film Genres:

Blaxploitation Films	Bollywood	French New Wave
Horror Films	Slasher Movies	Spaghetti Westerns
Vampire Films*	Film Noir	Heroic Bloodshed*

Film Subjects:

Laurel & Hardy	Marx Brothers	Animation
Steve McQueen*	Marilyn Monroe	The Oscars®
Filming On A Microbudget	Bruce Lee	Film Music

TV:

Doctor Who

Literature:

Cyberpunk	Philip K Dick	The Beat Generation
Agatha Christie	Sherlock Holmes	Noir Fiction*
Terry Pratchett	Hitchhiker's Guide	Alan Moore

Ideas:

Conspiracy Theories	Nietzsche	UFOs
Feminism	Freud & Psychoanalysis	

History:

Alchemy & Alchemists	The Crusades	The Black Death
Jack The Ripper	The Rise Of New Labour	Ancient Greece
American Civil War	American Indian Wars	

Miscellaneous:

- The Madchester Scene   Stock Market Essentials
  How To Succeed As A Sports Agent

Available at all good bookstores or send a cheque (payable to 'Oldcastle Books') to: **Pocket Essentials (Dept UFO), 18 Coleswood Rd, Harpenden, Herts, AL5 1EQ, UK.** £3.99 each (£2.99 if marked with an *) . For each book add 50p postage & packing in the UK and £1 elsewhere.